Postcard
from Palestine

SECOND EDITION

by Andrew Reid

 **MATTHIAS MEDIA**

Postcard from Palestine *Second edition*
First edition 1989
© Matthias Media, 1997

St Matthias Press Ltd. ACN 067 558 365
PO Box 225
KINGSFORD NSW 2032
AUSTRALIA
Ph: (02) 9663 1478   Fax: (02) 9662 4289
Email: sales@matthiasmedia.com.au
Web site: http://www.matthiasmedia.com.au

South African Distributor:
Christian Book Discounters
Ph: (021) 685 3663
Email: <peter@christianbooks.co.za>

ISBN 1 875245 57 X

Typesetting by Joy Lankshear Design Pty Ltd.

Table of Contents

page

Appendices

page

Getting started...

THE LIBRARIAN DISAPPEARED into some inner sanctum which the uninitiated like me could never enter. Minutes later, he appeared holding the huge tome. Carefully he placed it in front of me, watched me put on the white gloves, and left me to revel in the ancient splendour of a Wyclif Bible. This John Wyclif was the morning star of the English reformation. He and his followers were convinced of the importance of making the Bible available in English and so they gave us the first Bible in our language.

Today the spiritual descendants of Wyclif have given us such a bewildering array of Bibles in our own language that the Bible is now well and truly within the grasp of everyone. There are now Bibles for children, Bibles for students, Bibles for married people, Bibles that do all the work for you, right down to applying it for you. Yet, for many of us, the Bible is still a closed book. We have stopped reading and interpreting the Bible and left it to the experts, whether they be in the pulpit or in the ever-increasing margins of our Study Bibles.

This study guide is written with the conviction that the Bible is an open book for all. It is not for a special brand of people with inside knowledge. It is for us. We have minds and we have God's Spirit. We can be our own biblical interpreters. Moreover, it is written with the conviction that while diligent and hard work is needed to fathom the riches and wonders of God's word, the skills needed to accomplish this are easy to learn and available to anyone who is keen to learn.

It needs to be said that this study guide does not attempt to be a comprehensive guide to biblical interpretation and the science of biblical hermeneutics. If you are keen to learn more in these areas I have provided a graded reading list in an appendix. The list of books provided includes a section on the interaction between modern literary theory and biblical studies.

The structure of what follows is simple. I have devised a method of reading the Bible which covers the major principles of interpretation. The approach is to introduce these principles, provide some examples of them in action (the Examples section of each study), and then provide you with some exercises where you put the principles into action yourself (the 'Hands-On' section).

For my part, I'm going to work through the Old Testament book of Jonah in the Examples section, while you work through the New Testament book of Titus in the Hands-On section.

How to use this guide

Although individuals can certainly use this guide on their own, it is designed to be done under the supervision of someone skilled in biblical interpretation (e.g. a qualified leader in your church or parachurch organisation). If you intend working through the material in a group or course, we suggest that you have eight sessions of 60-90 minutes. The sessions are structured as follows:

SESSION	Section of *Postcard*	
1	Intro:	**Why bother with the Bible?**
2	Step 1:	**Depend on God for enlightenment**
3	Step 2:	**Form first impressions**
		2.1 Getting acquainted 2.2 Literary type 2.3 Structure
4	Step 3:	**Get background information**
		3.1 Geography 3.2 History
5	Step 4:	**Word meanings**
6	Step 5:	**Sum up your progress**
		5.1 Context 5.2 Summing up
7	Step 6:	**Determine other meanings**
		6.1 Links with other parts of the Bible 6.2 Biblical context
8	Step 7:	**Determine the impact**

If you are studying on your own

Read through the material in *Postcard From Palestine*, one session to a sitting. Try to summarise what you have read.

When you feel you have a good grasp of the ideas, turn to the Example where I work through Jonah. Read this as an example of how to put the principles discussed into practice. (**Warning**: some of the examples can seem pretty tough. They give you an indication of the sort of 'deep' study you can do, but it isn't expected that everyone will undertake this sort of analysis.) Then turn to the Hands-On section and work through the questions. You might find it helpful to show your work to an understanding friend, to get some feedback.

If you are studying in a group

Before each session each member should read the material for the coming session and work through the Hands-On exercises. Wide margins have been left for notes, questions and comments to be jotted throughout the text. Write your answers to the Hands-On material in this guide. This is a book to be written on.

When the group gets together, discuss your notes and questions from the text and the Examples, and compare answers for the Hands-On material.

If you are leading a group

If you are leading a group that is studying this book, then bearing the following things in mind will assist the group to run smoothly:

- Make sure everyone knows each other
- Start each session on time!
- Begin and/or end the meeting in prayer, asking for God's guidance in understanding and applying the material in each session.

- Encourage participation through inviting contributions to discussion and affirming people within the group. Don't let the more vocal or knowledgeable people dominate (this includes you!).
- Guide the discussion so that you stay on the topic. If there is a question you can't answer, then suggest somewhere the group can look for further information.
- Summarise the content of the study at the conclusion of each session.
- Finish each session on time!

The distinctive thing about this guide is its hands-on approach, and I cannot stress too strongly the importance of doing the Hands-On material. In fact, a large reason for revising this book was to make this activity more manageable than it was in the first edition. Breaking the bad reading habits of a Christian lifetime is not done easily or quickly. Put in the work now, and reap the benefits for years to come.

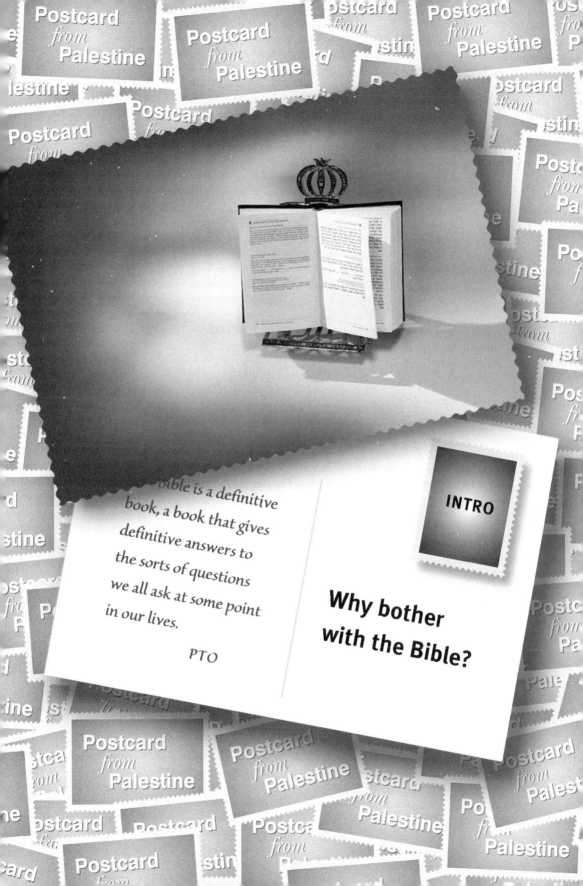

...ible is a definitive
book, a book that gives
definitive answers to
the sorts of questions
we all ask at some point
in our lives.

PTO

INTRO

Why bother
with the Bible?

THE BIBLE IS A DEFINITIVE BOOK, a book that gives definitive answers to the sorts of questions we all ask at some point in our lives.

> What is human life all about?
> Why is humanity's story such a puzzling combination of achievement and failure, goodness and badness, success and degradation?
> Where is the world going?
> Is there a god?
> What is God like?
> Can we relate to God?
> On what basis can we relate to God?
> Is life worth living?
> What sort of life ought we to live?
> Are there any standards we should be living up to?
> How is it possible to live up to them?

Rather than giving us packaged answers, the Bible addresses these great questions by telling us the story of God's dealings with his creation in general, and with humanity in particular. It makes some clear (and sometimes not so clear) statements about what God thinks about us and his creation.

However, the Bible is not only important because it answers the questions we ask. It is important because, as it tells stories and makes statements, it answers the questions that God thinks need answering. It does this most clearly when it reaches the climax of God's story of his dealings with humanity: the story of Jesus Christ. With the coming of Jesus and his death and resurrection, relationship between God and us is made possible. In Jesus it is possible to enjoy that relationship with God which God had intended from the beginning. This is why we bother with the Bible—it tells us about Jesus, about God, and about how to live in relationship with God. In the words of Paul, we bother with the Bible because its writings are "able to make you wise for salvation through faith in Christ Jesus" (2 Tim 3:15).

Clearing the Ground

The Bible: A book that everyone can read

The first point we need to bear in mind as we read the Bible is that it is perspicuous, meaning 'clear and lucid'. The Bible is intended to be (and can be) understood even by the most simple person because its essential content is clear and easily understood. The Bible is for all and is understandable by all. If you have an open Bible and a sound mind then you are equally as able to come to conclusions about what God is saying as the 'great ones'.

The Bible: A book that needs hard work

While the Bible is perspicuous and able to be understood by the most simple person, this does not mean that it is a simple book. It is a book from God, who is not simple, whose thoughts are far above our thoughts, whose wisdom and knowledge are deep and rich, whose judgements are unsearchable and whose ways are inscrutable (see Rom 11:33-36). Although almost anyone can understand the Bible, understanding the whole Bible and learning of the God who stands behind it will be a lifelong task requiring all that we have to give it.

The mention of hard work and a lifelong task puts up blocks immediately. Being the sinful people that we are, we want easy ways out. We want a sure-fire, time-saving way of reading the Bible that will guarantee results. There are no such shortcuts.

Avoiding hard work

Below I have listed some of the most common excuses for avoiding serious study of the Bible. Each excuse betrays one or more fundamental misunderstandings about the nature of God, or the Bible, or our own nature, or about the interaction that occurs between God and us as we go about interpreting the Bible.

"The Bible is self-explanatory and self-interpreting"

When people say this they generally mean that you don't need any aids to understand the Bible–that there is no need for outside help of any sort. There is a real element of truth to this proposition. As was said above, the Bible is perspicuous. It can be understood without aid by anyone who can read.

However, there is also some error in this view. This is apparent even at the most basic level. After all, the Bible is written in Hebrew, Aramaic and Greek and most of us don't know any of these languages. But even if we did, we couldn't understand those languages without reference to the culture in which they were developed. Every time we use an English translation, we depend on outside knowledge (in the shape of other documents which help us determine the meaning of the original languages).

At another level, some parts of the Bible are quite difficult to understand without bringing in outside material. A good example of this is Mark 13:14:

> *When you see 'the abomination that causes desolation' standing where it does not belong–let the reader understand–then let those who are in Judea flee to the mountains.*

Notice that the writer inserts an editorial comment in the speech of Jesus, urging the reader to understand–presumably this requires bringing in outside data, either from previous literature (e.g. the book of Daniel) or from past or contemporary incidents.

"I just pray and the Holy Spirit tells me what it means"

This is a common mistake in approaching Scripture. It is really a form of the first error just mentioned, and 1 Timothy 4 provides us with a helpful antidote against it (along with other references throughout 1 and 2 Timothy and Titus). These passages stress the need for diligence, faithfulness, seriousness and right handling of the truth in our study of Scripture.

As well as these encouragements in Scripture, closer examination reveals that this way of thinking doesn't stand up. Suppose for a moment that things really happened this way, and that merely by praying and glancing at the Bible we came to know what it means. If we pursue this to its logical conclusion, we must say that God has given me this meaning and that therefore it cannot be questioned (and must be true for everyone!). We end up with multitudes of Spirit-inspired interpreters and with no gauge by which to test them. The value of the Bible as an authoritative, God-breathed reference point is reduced to practically nothing. How will we ever know the truth?

"The mind is a bad thing"

There is amongst Christians today an underlying suspicion about the mind. Expressions such as that given above ("I just pray and the Holy Spirit tells me what it means") demonstrate that suspicion. We are in an anti-intellectual period of Christianity. There are numerous reasons for this. We are cynical about professional theologians and biblical scholars, who seem to compromise their belief in the truth for the sake of academic respectability. We feel swamped by the prejudice and ridicule of the world, and are often out-gunned in technical and philosophical learning. We have a deep-rooted fear that Christianity will not stand the test of intellectual scrutiny. Thus, it is common to find a massive disparity between our intellectual grasp of our own field or discipline while having a very shallow grasp of Christian truth.

We cannot succumb to this. Christianity is about relationships. But our relationship with God is established and maintained by God revealing himself to us. This revelation reaches its pinnacle in the person of Jesus and is recorded infallibly for us in the Scriptures. Christianity is therefore a religion of the book and books are apprehended primarily (though not exclusively) by our minds. What is more, the Bible will be able to stand the onslaught of our intellectual examination if God really is behind it!

The Guru syndrome

Throughout its history, Christianity has had problems with the fact that we, as human beings, often prefer the exciting to the mundane, and the experiential to the rational. This is reflected in how we judge those who speak the gospel to us. We tend to judge speakers on whether or not they are 'exciting' or 'spiritual'. Many of us push this even further by making such people 'gurus'. Swayed by their impressiveness, we depend upon them rather than upon God, the Holy Spirit, the Scriptures, or our own minds. To hear the following is not unusual:

> *"It's great going to my church and hearing our minister. The greatest thing about it is that if I ever have a problem with the Bible, I only have to go to the tape library at church. I know he will have spoken on it, and will have given an answer to my question. And most likely, he will be right."*

We don't have to restrict such comments to speakers. We can do the same with authors, publishers, and the like.

Again, there is an element of truth that needs to be affirmed here. God has greatly blessed us with gifted and godly older Christians, teachers and preachers who have insight and wisdom. It is right to listen to them and consult with them. They have been given their gifts to equip us for ministry, to help us grow in godliness, and to keep us from being tossed back and forward by every wind of doctrine (Eph 4:11-14). On the other hand, the Bible is clear in affirming that the mark of the new covenant is that each of us can know God ourselves and need not be dependent on people standing between us and God, acting as God for us (see Heb 8:8-12, which quotes Jer 31:31-34; also see 1 Jn 2:18-27)

Further, we need to recognise that all gurus stand on feet of clay. They all stumble in what they say and they are all not nearly as dependable as God, who reveals himself in the Scriptures and who gives us his Spirit (Jas 3:1-2; also see Acts 20:25-33). We could take a lesson from the Bereans in this regard. Upon hearing Paul preach, they went back to the authoritative Scriptures to test what he was saying (Acts 17:10-12).

Crucial elements in biblical interpretation

The Bible: The word of God

As Christians, we believe that the Bible is the word of God to humanity. It is inspired by him, a book from the hands of a divine author conveying timeless truths. Some of the implications of this are listed below.

- The Bible was not only written for one group of people a long time ago. It was also written "for us" (see Matt 22:31-32, where Jesus quotes Exod 3:6 to the Jews of first century Palestine).
- Because there is a divine author as well as a human author it may sometimes be that there are other meanings intended by God but not intended by the original author (1 Pet 1:10-13, 2 Pet 1:19-21).
- One piece of writing in the Bible does not stand on its own; it is part of a whole body of writing with the same divine author. There will be therefore various unifying strands running through it. The Bible 'hangs together'.
- True biblical interpretation must be done in dependence upon God for enlightenment. If we are to interpret the Bible accurately we must be in tune with the God who ultimately lies behind it. Our study of the Bible must be done in the context of prayer.
- The Bible will have implications for us today.
- We must stand under the Bible's authority. Studying the Bible is not merely an interesting academic exercise in history and sociology. It is listening to God speak. This means that we must not only depend on him for enlightenment, but also have receptive hearts and wills that are determined to obey what we hear.

The Bible: The word of a human author

As Christians, we believe that the Bible is also a human book in that it was written by human beings in human situations to other human beings in their own situation. If we combine this with the statements we made in the previous section we can say that *the Bible is a book with human authors that conveys timeless truths from God couched in human words.* This does not mean that the authors of the Bible were robots or automatons who lent their hands and pens to God. On the contrary, when each author wrote he had his own personality, his own history and his own way of expressing himself. Moreover, when he wrote he did so as a human being of his age, with various preconceptions concerning the nature of humanity, the world, and society. He wrote with the language and idiom of his surroundings to an audience who also held the various preconceptions of their age concerning the nature of humanity, the world, and society.

The implications of believing this are that our understanding of the Bible will be enhanced by finding out what we can of:

- the world, situation, history, personality and language of the original author and why he put the text together in the way that he did.
- the world, situation, history, personal details and language of the original reader/s.

In addition, determining the significance of the text for us will involve finding out what the text meant for the original hearer/s and what impact it might have had on them.

The text of Scripture

The writings of Scripture can at times appear quite different to the writings of our own world. They have their own forms, structure, genres and grammar. They are written in languages and affected by cultures far removed from our own. Moreover, God has used those languages and forms as a vehicle for conveying his word.

The implications of this are that we need to give ourselves to reading Scripture closely, taking these issues into account at least to some degree. We need to pursue the art of good reading, where we use the resources that are available to us in order to be as careful as possible with the Bible. While most of us can't give ourselves to the study of Hebrew, Aramaic, and Greek, it is possible to gain enough information about the language and world of the Scriptures in order to read the Bible in this careful way.

The reader/s of Scripture

However much we immerse ourselves in the world of the Bible, we will always be influenced in our reading habits by our own world. When we read Scripture, we enter into a kind of dialogue. That dialogue involves God, the original author, the original readers, and our point of accessing them all—the text of Scripture.

The implications of this for us as readers are as follows:

- Because God has chosen to reveal himself to us through other human beings in other contexts and in other times and places, we can't merely claim that a Bible text means *whatever it means to us.*

  We need to endeavour to understand what the text of Scripture might have meant in the *author's context* and what impact it might have had on them. As much as possible, what the Bible says to us should arise out of what the author said to his original hearers.

- We need to work out when our circumstances are similar to those of the author and original readers, and when they are different. Scripture itself guides us in making these decisions. It is possible that while the meaning of a particular passage may be no different for us and the original readers, the use we make of that Scripture and the impact it has on us will be affected by our circumstances.

A method for interpreting the Bible

The next few pages give us a way of interpreting the Bible which keeps in mind all the factors we have discussed. The seven steps of the method, and the principles on which they are based, form the structure for the units in the rest of this book. We work through the method together step by step, examining the principles, seeing them in action, and using them ourselves.

As we do this, it is important that we realise the deficiencies and artificiality of such a way of interpreting the Bible. We are not normally so 'formal' and structured in the way we read things. However, given that most of us have learnt bad ways of interpreting the Bible, it is necessary to relearn these basic skills in a structured way. The aim of using the method is to eventually make the process automatic—then you will be able to throw away the seven-step method.

Further, some parts of the method are not applicable to our interpretation of particular passages in the Bible. The passage we are studying will indicate this. For example, knowing the author, historical situation or items of geography may be totally unnecessary or impossible to determine in reading some of the wisdom books (i.e. Psalms, Proverbs, Ecclesiastes). In our normal everyday interpretation of communication we learn to sift, to ask questions, and not to apply unimportant questions. I trust that you will learn to do likewise with the Bible as you proceed. Here is a brief outline of the method.[1]

---

1   For further thoughts on some of the theoretical issues involved in interpretation, see the Appendix at the back of this book.

Step 1: Depend on God for enlightenment

Pray that God would be at work as you study his word, enlightening you and moving you towards faith in Christ and a life of obedience.

Step 2: Form first impressions

2.1 Getting acquainted

Reading through the section for first impressions.

2.2 Literary type

Find out what type of literature you are dealing with.

2.3 Structure

See if there are any indications within your chosen section of an order or structural pattern.

Step 3: Get background information

3.1 Geography

Ascertain whether the geographical setting is of importance to the meaning of the passage.

3.2 History

Find out whether the historical context is of importance to the meaning of the passage. Ask these questions:

The **Author:**
Is he identified?
Who is he?
What is his personal history?
What is his situation now?

The **Readers:**
Are they identified?
Who are they?
What is their history?
What is their situation now?

Contemporary History:
Are there any other current events at the time of writing which have relevance to the interpretation of the passage?

Step 4: Word meanings

Are there words which need further investigation? Find out what they mean in
        —their immediate context
        —the context of the book
        —the context of the writer
        —the context of its day
        —the context of its Testament
        —the context of the whole Bible.

Step 5: Sum up your progress

5.1 Context

Work out what place this passage plays in the thought of the surrounding passages and in the book as a whole.

5.2 Summing up

Draw together what you have learnt from the passage so far. This should help you get some idea of what the passage might have meant for the original readers. Some questions to ask are:
        —What did this passage tell the original readers about: God, the world, themselves and other people, the situations that they face?
        —What feelings and/or actions do you think it may have evoked in their particular situation?

Step 6: Determine other meanings

6.1 Links with other parts of the Bible

See if there are other passages in the Bible that have direct word, historical, theme, or thought links with this passage:

–within the author's other writings

–within the Testament

–within the whole Bible.

6.2 Biblical context

Determine what place this passage has in the thought of the whole Bible.

Step 7: Determine the impact

Sum up what you have learnt from the passage. Ask these questions:

–What does this passage tell us about God, the world, ourselves and other people, the situations that we face?

–Are there areas where I need to change my thinking as a result of what I've learnt?

–What feelings and/or actions should it evoke in my/our particular situation?

Finding a time and place

It should be immediately obvious that the type of Bible study we are talking about is not the sort of thing that is going to be easily squashed into a 20 minute daily Quiet Time. The best way forward is to continue reading the Bible the way we already do during our Quiet Time and set aside a more substantial regular time that we can give to concentrated Bible study for example, a one-hour spot on a regular basis when you can work hard at a particular passage or book of the Bible. Eventually, the skills you learn here will become automatic and begin to rub off on your daily reading of the Bible.

---

hands on

1. Think of your favourite novel. What do you appreciate most about it?

   i. the subject it deals with

   ii. the way it is written

   iii. what it tells you about the author

   iv. what the novel 'does' for you

How is your appreciation of the novel similar/different to your response to the Bible?

2. What truths follow from the fact that the Bible has:

   i. A divine author

   ii. Human authors

3. What problems can you detect with the following interpretations, given the principles we outlined in Study 1?

   a. In Isaiah 40:22, it says that "God sits enthroned above the circle of the earth". This is an indication that Bible writers thought the earth was spherical (cf Isaiah 11:12; Jeremiah 49:36; Matthew 24:31; Revelation 20:7).

   Sample answer to a: As twentieth century readers we know that the earth is spherical. This has been a relatively recent scientific discovery. To say that this verse proves that the Bible writers knew the earth to be spherical assumes that the author was not writing as a person of his times. Such an interpretation fails to take adequate account of the author and of the world he lived in and spoke to.

hands on

b. In Luke 10:1-12, Jesus commands his disciples to preach the gospel. This command is for us, too. This passage tells us how we are to preach the gospel and outlines the characteristics that will mark true preachers of the gospel.

c. Chapter 35 of Isaiah is God's promise that although I am going through a time of spiritual dryness at the moment it is not going to last. He is about to pour out his Spirit to bring new vitality and refreshment to my spiritual life.

d. Although the Bible condemns sex outside marriage as well as homosexuality, it only does so because it is reflecting the age and society in which it was written. The essence of the Bible is love and therefore it's quite okay to express our sexuality outside marriage today.

e. I've been reading my Bible and praying, and this morning while I was praying God spoke to me and made it very clear that it was right for me to leave my wife and divorce her.

hands on

f. Jesus says that God's first commandment is that we love him and the second is that we should love our neighbour as we love ourselves (Matt 22:34-40). It is clear from this that God wants us to love ourselves. It is a commandment from him. The reason that so many of us can't love our neighbour is that we haven't learnt to love ourselves.

g. The book of Revelation is a book about the end of the world. It's not much good me reading it. I'm not part of the final generation of the world.

h. 1 Corinthians 11 has nothing to say to me today. It is a chapter totally concerned with a first century situation that is irrelevant to us now.

Having grown up on the East coast of Australia I'd never seen the sun setting over the sea.

PTO

STEP
1

Depend on God for enlightenment

The God who is into communication

HAVING GROWN UP on the East coast of Australia I'd never seen the sun setting over the sea. And so when we settled in Perth it was with great anticipation that we wandered down to Scarborough Beach in Perth to buy our fish and chips and have a quick swim after yet another cloudless Western Australian summer day. Before long the sun dipped below waves clipped and foamed by the sea breeze and the deep blue framed a sky which grew from brilliant yellow and gold through to reds and crimsons before finally merging into blue and black studded by silver stars.

Since this first time we have returned time and time again. Sometimes we have watched the spectacle with gulls hovering in the breeze while we sit on the sand with our fish and chips. Other times we have walked with other spectators along nearby beaches watching while windsurfers skim the waves, trying to catch the last of the light. At other times we have sat drinking after-dinner cappuccinos in cafes overlooking the sea. And each time I have been filled with joy as I have heard the creation shout out to the world about its Creator. Each time I am staggered at God's creative activity. Each time I am drawn to worship him. And each time I am reminded of Psalm 19.

> *The heavens declare the glory of God;*
> *   the skies proclaim the work of his hands.*
> *Day after day they pour forth speech;*
> *   night after night they display knowledge.*
> *There is no speech or language*
> *   where their voice is not heard.*
> *Their voice goes out into all the earth,*
> *   their words to the ends of the world.*
> *In the heavens he has pitched a tent for the sun,*
> *   which is like a bridegroom coming forth from his pavilion,*
> *   like a champion rejoicing to run his course.*

It rises at one end of the heavens
  and makes its circuit to the other;
  nothing is hidden from its heat.

According to the Apostle Paul in Romans 1, my experience is a common one, for "since the creation of the world God's invisible qualities his eternal power and divine nature have been clearly seen, being understood from what has been made" (v.20). However, Paul also goes on to say that although we humans have heard God speak in his creation we uniformly "suppress the truth" and "become futile in out thinking and experience a darkening of our foolish hearts" (v.21). We do it, he says, by refusing to worship the Creator and turning instead to worship the things he has created. And we do it because of a deep-seated desire to be independent of him. The result of our disobedience and such wanton disregard for him is his anger. We are, says Paul in another letter, objects of God's wrath (Eph 2:3).

The rest of Paul's letter to the Romans tells us that God continues to speak to his world and that his clearest word is in his Son, Jesus Christ. In Jesus and his death God acts to bring us into right relationship with God "through faith in Jesus Christ". This right relationship is available "to all who believe".

This is God's great word to his world—the word which is Jesus Christ. It is this great word that is recorded for us infallibly in Scripture. In the Scriptures, God testifies about his Son Jesus and points us toward him. The Scriptures are God's inspired, infallible and sufficient word to us about Jesus, the only way to enter into relationship with God.

In Psalm 19, David captures this again. After exalting in God's revelation of himself in the created order, he turns to exalt in the clearer, more perfect revelation contained in the Scriptures.

The law of the Lord is perfect,
  reviving the soul.
The statutes of the Lord are trustworthy,
  making wise the simple.

Now if you think the sun setting over the sea is something to rejoice in and wonder at, how much greater is God's great word spoken clearly in Scripture. This explains David's overflowing praise:

> *The precepts of the Lord are right,*
>   *giving joy to the heart...*
> *They are more precious than gold,*
>   *than much pure gold;*
> *they are sweeter than honey,*
>   *than honey from the comb.*

Psalm 119 is also full of this sort of language. We read words such as 'rejoice', 'delight', and 'love'. The reading of the Scriptures doesn't appear to be a duty or a burden here, rather a privilege and a source of great comfort, encouragement, joy and longing. Rather than finding reading or hearing God's word a drudgery,

---

example

Here are some helpful models from Scripture and elsewhere that capture the right sorts of attitudes and approach to reading the Bible.

Do good to your servant, and I will live; I will obey your word. Open my eyes that I may see wonderful things in your law. (Ps 119:17-18)

I keep asking that the God of our Lord Jesus Christ, the glorious Father, may give you the Spirit of wisdom and revelation, so that you may know him better. I pray also that the eyes of your heart may be enlightened in order that you may know the hope to which he has called you, the riches of his glorious inheritance in the saints, and his incomparably great power for us who believe. (Eph 1:17-19)

Blessed Lord, you have caused all holy Scriptures to be written for our learning: grant us so to hear them, read, mark, learn, and inwardly digest them, that, encouraged and supported by your holy Word, we may embrace and always hold fast the joyful hope of everlasting life, which you have given us in our Saviour Jesus Christ. (From the Anglican *Book of Common Prayer*)

Heavenly Father, give us faith to receive your word, understanding to know what it means, and the will to put it into practice; through Jesus Christ our Lord. (From the Anglican *Book of Common Prayer*)

David finds the absence of God's word an intolerable burden.

The Psalmist has this attitude because he knows that true life is life lived in the light of God's advice and instruction. Therefore, although God's word sometimes exposes and threatens him, he knows that it can only bring him good. Hence he rejoices in reading it.

Unfortunately, for some of us the sense of delight and wonder at the Almighty God speaking directly to us under the inspiration of the Holy Spirit through the pages of Scripture has gone. We have forgotten that while the Scriptures are telling us of Jesus, the otherwise unknown and unknowable God is making himself known. We no longer come to the Scriptures in full expectation that as we read and think and meditate on them God will come and speak to us. A proper grasp of the doctrine of the inspiration of Scripture should remedy this and change our attitude.

My hope as you work through this book is that your experience will be fed by the doctrine of the inspiration of Scripture.

These sample prayers are not meant to give the impression that we just need to murmur a few words before we open our Bibles. Rather, the whole process of interpreting the Bible must be saturated with prayer. From beginning to end, we must read with God in mind. After we have finished our study, we should meditate on what we have learnt and ask God to help us see how we should change our attitudes and actions.

There is a Scriptural example of this in action in Daniel 9. Daniel is struggling with the application of the Scriptures (in this case, the prophecies of Jeremiah) to his own situation and the situation of his nation as a whole. In verse 3, he tells us that as he grappled with these Scriptures he "turned to the Lord God and pleaded with him in prayer and petition, in fasting, in sackcloth and ashes".

It is in the context of such prayer that God explains to him what the prophecy of seventy years means and how it applies in his own day. Here is someone who understands an original Scripture written to an original context and group of people, who realises that what Scripture says is for him as well as the original hearers, and who therefore earnestly seeks the Author of Scripture for further enlightenment and application. Here is a model interpreter at work.

As you learn better ways of reading your Bible, you will hear the living God speaking to you in stronger and clearer ways and your relationship with him will thereby be deepened.

Getting our Bible reading in context

I love books. I would gladly be shut up in a library for the rest of my life merely to read everything I could get my hands on. In my ideal world, I would be surrounded by things to read and by the ideas contained in them.

The Christian faith both feeds my love of books and blows it apart. On the one hand, Christianity is a religion that is concerned with books and therefore with my mind. It tells me that if I am to know God then I must acquaint myself with his self-revelation in Christ, which is spoken about in an inspired book.

On the other hand, Christianity goes far beyond the pages of the Bible and forces me out from my desk. It is a religion that is bound up with relating to living people and to God; to the world he has made and to the people he has made to live in it. The great and first commandment is not "Read a book about God and become acquainted with ideas about him" but "You shall love the Lord your God with all your heart, soul, strength and mind" and the second commandment is like it, "You shall love your neighbour as yourself". Reading the Bible may be how I get to know who God is, what he is like, what he has done for me and what he demands of me, but God intends that this knowledge should infiltrate my whole being, changing the way I relate to him and others.

So right from the beginning we must make sure that God is involved in our interpretation of the Bible. It must not become an intellectual exercise divorced from him.

Gaining access to the divine author

As we said above, even before we sit down to study the Bible, God has been involved. He so inspired the Bible writers through the Holy Spirit that, as they wrote, they spoke from God (2 Peter 1:20-21; cf. 1 Timothy 3:16). He, working through the human authors, is the divine author of Scripture.

Now although we cannot have direct access to the human authors, we can have direct access to the divine author. If we are Christians, then we have the same Holy Spirit who inspired the passages we are reading. He knows what God wants us to understand from the Bible and, as we depend on him, he will lead us into the truth and help us to obey it.

Before we start, then, we need to pray. We need to come before God, acknowledging our need for him to reveal himself to us and to help us interpret and apply what we read. We need him to enlighten us, to show us how we need to change and to melt our resistance to do his will. We need to ask him to help us understand, remember, love and obey what we learn from the Scriptures so that we might live in a way that pleases him. The people who read the Bible this way are the ones whom God esteems (Isaiah 66:2).

hands on

1. Read through Psalm 19 and Romans 1:18-25 and put the argument of each passage in your own words:

Psalm 19

Romans 1:18-25

2. If you haven't done so yet, stop, put down this book and spend some time praying about how you read the Bible. Pray about your attitudes, your current Bible reading practices (or lack of them) and your desire to know God better. Ask him to open your mind to his word as you learn to study it more deeply using this guide.

3. Write down your name on a piece of paper. Under your name write down one area in your attitude to Bible reading or in your practice of Bible reading that you would like to see improved. Distribute the sheets of paper randomly in the group and commit yourself to praying for that person throughout the history of the group.

In getting under way,
the first and most obvious
thing you need to do
is to pick a book of the
Bible to study.

PTO

STEP 2

Form first impressions

Step 2.1: Getting acquainted

Choose a book

In getting under way, the first and most obvious thing you need to do is to pick a book of the Bible to study. To start with, choose one that is not too difficult or long (e.g. a Psalm, Obadiah, Malachi, Galatians, 1 Peter, James). Later, you can use the methods outlined here to look at larger books or parts of books. In this guide, we will look at the short books of Jonah and Titus.

Get acquainted with the book

Before you start serious study of a passage or section, aim to read through the book you are going to study two or three times. For some of us who are used to reading only short sections of the Bible the idea of reading whole books can be a bit daunting. However, it might be good to start thinking a bit more freely and realistically. After all, most of Paul's letters are not much longer than the Christmas letters we get from our friends and read in a few minutes each year. Some of the Old Testament narrative sections are a lot shorter than some of the novels we read, and sometimes more exciting and vigorous. Rather than being daunted that we might not understand, we can approach each book we study knowing that before long it will become an old friend to us. Knowing this, we can be free to just flow with the book, reading it somewhat as we would a letter we know we are going to come back to in more detail later.

The first time through, read the book from beginning to end without stopping. The second time through, do the same with a pen in hand, jotting down your first impressions of the book. The sorts of things to record include which parts strike you, what reactions you have to it, what areas of life it appears to address, what questions it raises and what mood it is written in.

Make up an outline of the book

The aim of the third reading is to make a provisional outline of the structure of the book. We want to see how the author has laid out his material and how each part is related to the other. Don't forget that the original author didn't put in the chapter breaks, verse numbers or headings. All these have been added by people endeavouring to be helpful.

The following notes give some guidelines as to how to go about this process with a smaller book, such as Jonah or Titus. In case you want to try a larger book later on, the principles are the same, just on a larger scale.

---

example

Here are the notes I took as I got acquainted with the book of Jonah. On reading it through the second time I asked myself:

Why is Jonah so rebellious?
What's Jonah's view of God?
How is it that Jonah doesn't act like other prophets when he is called?
What would I do in Jonah's situation?
The picture of God is striking: He is powerful, compassionate, caring to both Jews and pagans, etc.
Is it right to talk to God the way Jonah does?
Jonah has a freedom in interacting with God that I'd be scared to exercise. Am I wrong or is Jonah wrong?
I really like the book. It's punchy and down to earth. In a funny way I like Jonah too. He's easy to identify with. Why?
What is the Psalm doing there?
Who are the heroes in the book (Jonah, the mariners, or the Ninevites)?
Did this really happen?
What's this business about the fish?

On reading Jonah through for the third time, I thought that the chapter divisions in my English Bible were basically right. The book could be divided into four sections. The first two sections concerned Jonah and his flight from God and his word. The second two sections concerned Nineveh and its acceptance of God's word. Both sections have a rescue or deliverance (Jonah in chapter 2; the Ninevites in chapter 3). A draft outline might go as follows:

1:1-2:10	**Jonah at sea**
1:1-17	*Fleeing and fearing God.*
2:1-10	*God rescues Jonah*
3:1-4:11	**Jonah at Nineveh**
3:1-10	*God rescues Nineveh*
4:1-11	*Disputing God's generosity*

Having drawn up this outline, I went to a Bible dictionary and a commentary. The *New Bible Dictionary* doesn't actually give an outline but agrees that the four chapter divisions are right and that these divisions neatly divide the subject matter. The Tyndale commentary divides the book as follows:

1:1-2:10	**Jonah at sea**

For smaller books:
- Look for major divisions (notice breaks in thought, connecting words and changes in person).
- Give a title to each that clearly states the content of the section.
- Look for natural subdivisions. Follow the same procedure as above, if possible making the title of the subdivision relate to the title of the major division.

Consult a commentary or Bible dictionary.

Most commentaries or Bible dictionaries give an outline of the structure of a book. Compare yours with theirs. Don't automatically assume that they are right! Adjust your outline as you see fit.

Of course, you could have done this at the start and saved yourself a lot of trouble, but you would not have gained a feel for the book yourself, nor would you have read the Bible yourself (which is the purpose of this whole exercise).

Take one of your divisions for detailed study

If you are studying the whole book then it is obviously best to start with the first of your sections (that is, about a chapter or so in length). If you are only wanting to study one section of a book (e.g. Isaiah 53) then take that passage. Now you are ready to get started on the detailed study of Scripture.

---

example

1:1-3	*Jonah's initial call*	The difference in the two break-ups of the book seems
1:4-16	*Jonah and the sailors*	minor and there is probably no reason to change my
1:17-2:10	*Jonah's gratitude for his own*	own break-up. Further detailed analysis of the book
	deliverance	will help in working out if I should make any changes
		If we were studying a larger book, then at this
3:1-4:11	**Jonah at Nineveh**	point I'd take one of my sections (e.g. chapters 1 and
3:1-3	*Jonah's second call*	2) for more detailed study and analyse each of the
3:4-10	*Jonah and the Ninevites*	sections in order. Since Jonah is such a small book we
4:1-11	*Jonah's anger at Nineveh's deliverance*	will look at the whole book in one go.

Step 2.2: Literary type

"Is the Bible Fact or Fiction? Archaeologists in the Holy Land are shedding new light on tales of the Scriptures"
"Sex on the Internet"
"Cricketer fears for life at World Cup"

I'm standing in the newsagent, trying not to get sucked in by the headlines. Opting for a newspaper and the magazine with the article on the Bible, I return to the cool of my car to eat lunch and skim-read the Bible article. A quick glance tells me that there's not much new light being shed. The evidence hasn't changed much since I last read up on it and many of the arguments still seem to rest on speculations by historians that are not unanimously agreed upon in academic circles. Rationalising that I've still got the rest of the magazine to read and therefore my money hasn't been wasted, I pick up the paper and flip over to 'Hagar the Horrible' and then to an editorial on the latest balance of payment figures.

We have learnt, by practice and education, to automatically engage a particular gear as we read. When we read headlines, we have learnt to be suspicious of them until we read the first page. When we see "Sex on the Internet" on a *Playboy* billboard, we have a fair idea what is inside. On opening the paper and reading the comics, our minds engage another gear which enjoys and yet does not believe for a moment that there is a real Hagar the Horrible. Our minds switch to a serious, reflective mood as we read the editorial, again because our experience tells us that this literature is far different from the comics and ought to be treated differently.

Spy novels, satire, fantasy, computer manuals, newspapers– these are all quite different kinds, or 'genres', of writing. We approach each of these genres in a particular way and adopt different attitudes to them as we read. In a sense, our minds have been conditioned to read in this way. Sometimes libraries help us by categorising their literature into various classifications or by putting dust-jackets on books to help us identify them.

Such thinking about literature is helpful for us when we approach the Bible. The Bible is the literary library of a nation, housing a host of different literary types.

Unfortunately, we have usually been taught to read the Bible in only one gear, usually the one in which we read the Epistles of Paul. But if we are going to understand what the original author wanted to say to the original hearers we must:

- recognise that there are a variety of literary genres in the Bible.
- learn to identify these genres.
- become acquainted with these various genres and the different ways of reading them.
- change the way we read as we come across these different literary types.

In other words we must learn to read prose as prose, poetry as poetry, history as history, fiction as fiction, letter as letter and prophecy as prophecy. We must avoid treating poetry as prose (and vice versa), history as fiction (and vice versa). To do otherwise would be as crazy as reading an Alistair Maclean novel as history, or a romance as true life!

Some common literary genres

Here are some of the most common literary genres in the Scriptures:

poetry	law
gospel	prophecy
narrative	epistle
psalm	court epic
history	fictional tale
drama	parable
apocalyptic	

Although it is helpful to recognise that the Bible is made up of different literary genres, we need to be careful that we don't classify too tightly. Genres can be a bit fuzzy-edged. For example, prophecy is very commonly written in poetic terms; gospel and epistle often contain sections of apocalyptic; parables are often found within the larger literary genre of gospel; the Psalms contain laments, hymns and thanksgivings.

In the last few years some good introductory books have been written on identifying and interpreting literary genres. These books are listed in the reading list under 'Genre analysis and interpretation' in the *Further Reading* appendix at the end of the book. Another way ahead is to gradually read a bible dictionary articles on some of the main genres listed above (e.g. parable, apocalyptic, prophecy).

example

On reading through Jonah, the question of genre immediately pushes itself to the front. At one level, the book occurs among all the other prophetic books, thereby inclining us to treat it as prophecy. But then again it doesn't look or feel like the books that surround it. There are no tell-tale "thus says the Lord" statements, only part of it is written poetically and there is a large percentage of narrative.

At another level, there are some elements of seeming exaggeration and perhaps even unreality (e.g. the fish, the size of Nineveh, the repentance of Nineveh, etc.). It's not too hard to see why some people consider the book to be a parable.

While these issues may not be of fundamental significance to the interpretation of the text, they are of some importance. For example, if the book is a parable then we will need to think more about other meanings that may underlie the text and the people represented in the text.

So, how do we resolve these difficulties? My way ahead is to write down two headings and to jot down my thoughts under them.

1. What are the major arguments in favour of the work being imaginative/ fictional rather than historical?

• *The story is just so incredible at times. I think that if I gave it to some of my friends at work they'd say that things like this just don't happen. Big fish don't swallow people and spit them out alive after three days. Whole cities don't repent just because some wandering Jewish prophet tells them that God has it in for them. Trees don't grow overnight except in fairy stories like Jack and the Beanstalk.*

• *The writer seems to exaggerate everything.*

2. What are the major arguments in favour of the book being considered as a work of history/ prophecy?

• *From what I remember, Jesus seems to talk as though Jonah really existed and the events that are recorded actually happened. My browsing through a commentary indicates that it's only recently that people have doubted that the book is historical. Surely ancient authorities are more likely to be familiar with this type of literature and how it should be treated.*

Step 2.3: Structure

At the moment there is a small plastic box sitting beside our refrigerator full of coloured magnetic letters. It has been years since it was used but at one time it was a standard toy for every member of our family. Some of the older ones in the family used to write love notes to each other or sentences of affectionate defamation. The younger members put the letters together to form patterns of colour or shapes and eventually patterns that became words and sentences. No matter who we are, the plastic bucket beside the refrigerator is an opportunity to express our human desire to put order and structure into things and, in so doing, to make chaos take on meaning.

Without structure, writing has no meaning, in the same way that coloured magnetic letters have no meaning until they are put together. It is the way that we put them together than gives meaning. So the letters 'o', 'g' and 'd' can be put together nonsensically ('ogd') or they can be put together as 'god' or 'dog'. On a larger scale, the words 'loves', 'George', and 'Mildred' on their own mean very little but rearranging them and giving them structure suddenly conveys meaning and even offers different possibilities

---

example

• *It's not as though the events in Jonah are that strange compared with other stories of the prophets or other people in the Old Testament. For example these things seem to happen in the book of Judges and in the stories about Elijah in 1 Kings 17-19.*

My conclusion was to be cautious and to treat the book as it presents itself and as those who put it in the canon of Scripture categorised it—that is, as the story of a particular set of circumstances in the life of a Jewish prophet. These were recorded because of their unusual nature and because of the key things those events teach about God and his way of working in his world. In other words, I decided to consider it as prophecy tied into history rather than fiction.

Having decided this, it will be important for me to keep my mind open when I get to do more detailed work on the book. Close work on its text should continue to advise and revise my opinions and I should be open to change if the passage itself points in that direction.

of meaning. Meaning is very much conveyed by the way letters, words, sentences, paragraphs, chapters and ideas are put together.

Most of the time the structure of what we say is unconscious. However, sometimes it is deliberate and very conscious. Either way, the structure of what we say conveys information about ourselves and forms part of what we want to say.

Psalm 119 is a very good Scriptural example of the use of structure to convey meaning and to give added emphasis to the content. The first thing the Hebrew reader notices is that the author has a very definite structure in mind. The poem is an acrostic: the first eight verses begin with the first letter of the Hebrew alphabet; the second eight verses begin with the second letter of the alphabet; and so on, through the whole Hebrew alphabet. The whole psalm, in terms of content, is a praise of the law, the word of God, and the joys to be found in keeping it. By setting out the psalm in this way, the author reminds us of the fullness of the word of God and that it is the essence of all of life.

Although Paul sometimes seems to get carried away in his arguments and begins to extol God or go off on a tangent, his letters also reveal a structure that is very important in understanding his writing. For example, on a broad level, you will often find that Paul spends the first half of a letter spelling out the gospel before drawing out its implications for the lives of his hearers. This move from doctrine to its implications (and his exhortation to change) is often heralded by the word 'therefore' (as in Rom 12:1-2; Eph 4:1; Col 3:1). This structuring of his letters tells us important things about Paul's understanding of the basis for Christian ethical decisions: they are to be based on the gospel; on what God has done for us in Christ.

Whether conscious or unconscious, the way a writer has structured what he says communicates meaning and gives impact. Analysing structure will therefore be an important part of determining what the original author intended to say to the original readers/hearers, and how he intended them to react to what he said. Remember that structures can be quite prominent (e.g. Ps 119), or quite unobtrusive (e.g. parts of the Gospels), but are quite often significant.

There are various levels of structure in the Bible. At the top end we have the structure of the Bible itself, which tells us a lot about how people viewed its contents and how they thought it ought to be read. Other levels include major sections within the book (e.g. Gen 1-11; 12-50), smaller sections (e.g. chapters), sentences and phrases.

The aim of this section is to develop principles for analysing the structure of Bible passages. The importance of sentence structure will be covered in Step 4 on Meaning.

Presuming we have broken a book into smaller, manageable sections for more detailed study, what should we do and what should we look for? [1]

Look for patterns within the passage

Photocopy the passage and invest in some coloured pens. Use them to mark in the following:

- repetitions of words and ideas (e.g. 'grace', 'faith', etc)
- changes in the person being talked about (e.g. changes from 'he/she' to 'I' or 'you', or from 'they' to 'me' or 'you')
- ideas that are dropped and then resumed later
- central or pivotal words, ideas, or events
- comparisons (i.e. the association of similar things or ideas, such as, 'as wise as serpents')
- contrasts (i.e. the association of opposite things or ideas, such as, 'light or darkness')

In all of this, the key elements are 'repetition' and 'progression' (i.e. where a word or idea is developed progressively through the passage). By way of example, read 2 Corinthians 1:3-11 below.

> *Blessed be the God and Father of our Lord Jesus Christ, the Father of mercies and the God of all consolation, who consoles*

---

1   For this exercise, as for all detailed work on a passage, you should use a more literal translation of the Bible such as the New American Standard Bible. For more information on translations and why some are to be preferred for this sort of work, see the appendix on Bible translations.

us in all our affliction, so that we may be able to console those who are in any affliction with the consolation with which we ourselves are consoled by God. For just as the sufferings of Christ are abundant for us, so also our consolation is abundant through Christ. If we are being consoled, it is for your consolation, which you experience when you patiently endure the same sufferings that we are also suffering. Our hope for you is unshaken; for we know that as you share in our sufferings, so also you share in our consolation.

We do not want you to be unaware, brothers and sisters, of the affliction we experienced in Asia; for we were so unutterably, unbearably crushed that we despaired of life itself. Indeed, we felt that we had received the sentence of death so that we would rely not on ourselves but on God who raises the dead. He who rescued us from so deadly a peril will continue to rescue us; on him we have set our hope that he will rescue us again, as you also join in helping us by your prayers, so that many will give thanks on our behalf for the blessing granted us through the prayers of many.

Which words in the passage are repeated? Which words are central? Notice the frequent change from 'you' and 'your' to 'us', 'our' or 'we'. Notice how the word 'affliction' occurs at the beginning of the passage, how it is then dropped only to be taken up later. There is also a comparison between God's raising the dead and his rescuing Paul from his affliction.

Look for the natural flow of the passage

With pen in hand, ask yourself:

- How does the passage start?
- How does it proceed?
- How does it come to an end?
- Does the structure seem to bear any relation to the meaning or impact of the passage?
- Is there any inherent logic to the passage?

Again, this can be illustrated with the passage from 2 Corinthians 1. Paul starts by talking about God's consolation of all his afflictions. He then reflects on how both consolation and affliction appear to be a necessary part of being Christian and that they have a beneficial spin-off for others. In the second paragraph, Paul illustrates his point by talking about his own experience before reflecting on it theologically and drawing out its practical implications. In many ways the whole passage is simply an expansion of the first verse which blesses God as the 'Father of mercies' and 'God of all consolation'.

Put all your findings together

Ask yourself (again, jotting down your thoughts and conclusions):

- What is the passage emphasising?
- Why has the writer ordered the words and ideas the way he has?
- What is being stressed?
- Is there anything that really stands out about the structure (e.g. elements that are beautiful, striking, jarring, offensive, unexpected, unique)?

Perhaps a 'flow chart' of the thoughts of the passage might be a good way of putting this all together. Alternatively, you can try summarizing the passage in a few short sentences. We've already done most of this with regard to 2 Corinthians 1:3-11.

If appropriate, reflect your findings in a break-up of the passage

That is, work out some headings for the various sections of the passage that help demonstrate the structure of the passage. (Remember that your headings, like those put in by some Bibles, are not part of the Bible) My break-up of our 2 Corinthians passage would be to put in two headings. I'd label the first paragraph 'Thanks to the God of all consolation' while the second I'd label 'Who delivered me from a deadly peril'.

Compare your findings with a commentary

Look up a commentary or Bible dictionary and see if their analysis gives you any fresh insights. Change your findings if you think it is necessary, but don't feel compelled to bow before the authority of the commentator.

Some cautions:

Be careful!

Structure *is* a device often used by the author to convey meaning and make an impact. Structure *can be* an aid for the interpreter to determine meaning and impact. But don't force structure where it is not intended to be. Not every passage has a neat structure.

---

example

We've already seen how to arrive at a simple structure for a passage like 2 Corinthians 1. This sort of structural analysis can be taken further. My section for study here was Jonah 1. On reading through the chapter I noticed some elements that made me wonder if the author had structured the chapter in a particular way.

God speaks his word to Jonah
Jonah hears the word and refuses to obey
The Lord hurls a great wind and there
    is a great storm
The sailors become afraid
The sailors cry to their gods
The sailors act to save themselves
Jonah sleeps to avoid the storm
The sailors question Jonah
Jonah responds and says he 'worships'
    (NASB has 'fears') the Lord

The sailors are afraid
The sailors question Jonah again
Jonah tells them that they can avoid the storm
    by throwing him overboard
The sailors try to save Jonah and themselves
    by rowing
The sailors pray to the Lord
The sailors fear the Lord and honour him.
God rescues Jonah.

While the structure is not neat, the progress is evident. The story is framed around words for 'throwing' and 'fearing' and also around the actions of the participants (God, Jonah, the sailors). This framing of the story points to the central verses being verses 9 and 10, where Jonah says he 'fears' the Lord but where the sailors' fear seems to be more than just words.

Don't miss the point!

Our aim is not to atomise the text so that it loses its impact. The structure must be left intact so that its force upon us is maintained.

Don't overdo it!

Those of us who like toying with words, analyzing structural patterns, and playing with coloured pencils and highlighters, need to realize that structure is but one means the author can use. Some authors convey meaning and impact by painting pictures in words for us. Their writing is often loose and unstructured. To tighten it up would be to destroy it. Sometimes you may find both loose and tight writing within the same book. The book of Revelation, for example, relies heavily on both structure and imagery.

---

example

When I checked out these thoughts in a commentary I found that other people had noticed the structure of the chapter and there had been some detailed work done on it. The one that reflected my own work, but also added some detail I had missed, was that offered by Alexander in the Tyndale Old Testament Commentary on *Obadiah, Jonah, and Micah* (Leicester: IVP, 1988).

A Yahweh hurls a wind on the sea; the storm begins; sailors fear and cry to their gods (vv 4-5)

  B Jonah sleeps; cry to your god; we shall not perish; divine sovereignty (vv 5b-6)

    C that we may know on whose account (v 7)

      D the sailors question Jonah (v 8)

        E I fear (v 9)

        E¹ the sailors fear (v 10)

      D¹ the sailors question Jonah (v 11)

    C¹ I know that it is on my account (v 12)

  B¹ sailors strive for land; sailors cry to Yahweh; let us not perish; divine sovereignty (vv 13-14)

A¹ sailors hurl Jonah into sea; the storm ceases; sailors fear Yahweh and sacrifice (vv 15-16)

hands on

1. What genre of Bible literature do you find the most difficult? Why?

2. Why is it important to work out what literary genre you are dealing with in the Bible?

3. Think of your favourite movie or novel (or even a sermon you have heard recently). Can you outline its structure, like you did for 2 Corinthians? What part do you think the structure plays in the impact the book/film/sermon has upon you?

Step 2.1: Getting acquainted

4. At the end of this chapter you will find the book of Titus typed out. Read it through three times in the manner suggested above, recording relevant notes and devising your own outline, complete with headings. Check out your outline with a commentary or Bible dictionary. Remember, Titus is a small book, so you are looking for major divisions and natural subdivisions. You are not trying to break it up in great detail. We will do that later.

Step 2.2: Literary type

5. Following is a list of genres. Indicate whether each one can be found in Titus. How did you come to your decisions?

history	y/n	fiction	y/n
poetry	y/n	apocalyptic	y/n
law	y/n	psalm	y/n
prophecy	y/n	proverb	y/n
epistle	y/n		

Step 2.3: Structure

6. For the rest of our time we are going to concentrate on Titus 2. Using the methods outlined in Step 2.3, analyse the structure of this chapter (or your closest major division that takes in this chapter). Feel free to write in this book with pens, highlighters or coloured pencils. We have left plenty of space around the text for this purpose. If you prefer, photocopy some extra copies and work on those.

TITUS

Paul, a servant of God and an apostle of Jesus Christ, for the sake of the faith of God's elect and the knowledge of the truth that is in accordance with godliness, in the hope of eternal life that God, who never lies, promised before the ages began in due time he revealed his word through the proclamation with which I have been entrusted by the command of God our Saviour, to Titus, my loyal child in the faith we share: Grace and peace from God the Father and Christ Jesus our Saviour. I left you behind in Crete for this reason, so that you should put in order what remained to be done, and should appoint elders in every town, as I directed you: someone who is blameless, married only once, whose children are believers, not accused of debauchery and not rebellious. For a bishop, as God's steward, must be blameless; he must not be arrogant or quick-tempered or addicted to wine or violent or greedy for gain; but he must be hospitable, a lover of goodness, prudent, upright, devout, and self-controlled. He must have a firm grasp of the word that is trustworthy in accordance with the teaching, so that he may be able both to preach with sound doctrine and to refute those who contradict it. There are also many rebellious people, idle talkers and deceivers, especially those of the circumcision; they must be silenced, since they are upsetting whole families by teaching for sordid gain what it is not right to teach. It was one of them, their very own prophet, who said, Cretans are always liars, vicious brutes, lazy gluttons. That testimony is true. For this reason rebuke them sharply, so that they may become sound in the faith, not paying attention to Jewish myths or to commandments of those who reject the truth. To the pure all things are pure, but to the corrupt and unbelieving nothing is pure. Their very minds and consciences are corrupted. They profess to know God, but they deny him by their actions. They are detestable, disobedient, unfit for any good work. But as for you, teach what is consistent with sound doctrine. Tell the older men to be temperate, serious, prudent, and sound in faith, in love, and in endurance. Likewise, tell the older women to be reverent in behaviour, not to be slanderers or slaves to drink; they are to teach what is good, so that they may encourage the young women to love their husbands, to love their children, to be self-controlled, chaste, good managers of the household, kind, being submissive to their husbands, so that the word of God may not be discredited. Likewise, urge the younger men to be self-controlled. Show yourself in all respects a model of good works, and in your teaching show integrity, gravity, and sound speech that cannot be censured; then any opponent will be put to shame, having nothing evil to say of us. Tell slaves to be submissive to their masters and to give satisfaction in every respect; they are not to talk back, not to pilfer, but to show complete and perfect fidelity, so that in everything they may be an ornament to the doctrine of God our Saviour. For the grace of God has appeared, bringing salvation to all, training us to renounce impiety and worldly passions, and in the present age to live lives that are self-controlled, upright and godly, while we wait for the blessed hope and the manifestation of the glory of our great God and Saviour, Jesus Christ. He it is who gave himself for us that he might redeem us from all iniquity and purify for himself a people of his own who are zealous for good deeds. Declare these things; exhort and reprove with all authority. Let no one look down on you. Remind them to be subject to rulers and authorities, to be obedient, to be ready for every good work, to speak evil of no one, to avoid quarrelling, to be gentle, and to show every courtesy to everyone. For we ourselves were once foolish, disobedient, led astray, slaves to various passions and pleasures, passing our days in malice and envy, despicable, hating one another. But when the goodness and loving kindness of God our Saviour appeared, he saved us, not because of any works of righteousness that we had done, but according to his mercy, through the water of rebirth and renewal by the Holy Spirit. This Spirit he poured out on us richly through Jesus Christ our Saviour, so that, having been justified by his grace, we might become heirs according to the hope of eternal life. The saying is sure. I desire that you insist on these things, so that those who have come to believe in God may be careful to devote themselves to good works; these things are excellent and profitable to everyone. But avoid stupid controversies, genealogies, dissensions, and quarrels about the law, for they are unprofitable and worthless. After a first and second admonition, have nothing more to do with anyone who causes divisions, since you know that such a person is perverted and sinful, being self-condemned. When I send Artemas to you, or Tychicus, do your best to come to me at Nicopolis, for I have decided to spend the winter there. Make every effort to send Zenas the lawyer and Apollos on their way, and see that they lack nothing. And let people learn to devote themselves to good works in order to meet urgent needs, so that they may not be unproductive. All who are with me send greetings to you. Greet those who love us in the faith. Grace be with all of you.

(From the New Revised Standard Version)

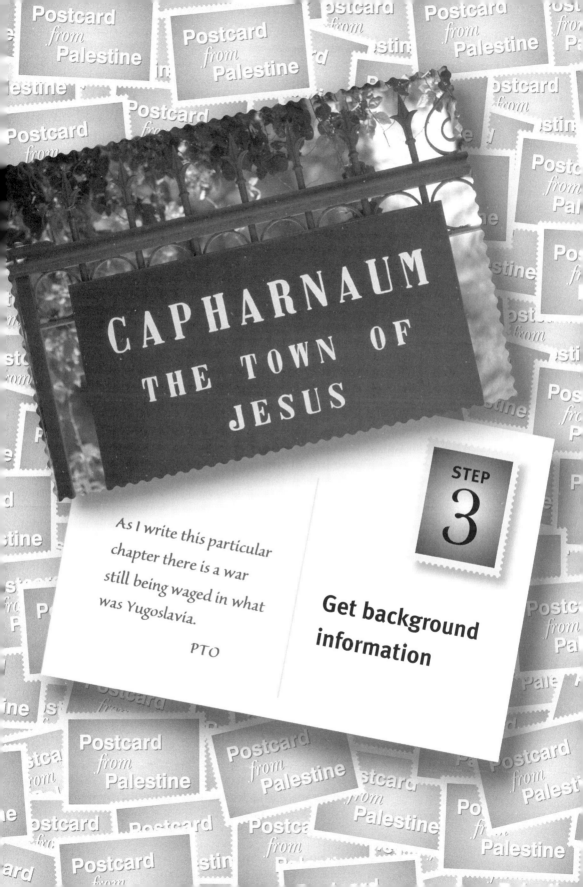

CAPHARNAUM
THE TOWN OF JESUS

As I write this particular chapter there is a war still being waged in what was Yugoslavia.

PTO

STEP
3

Get background information

AS I WRITE THIS particular chapter there is a war still being waged in what was Yugoslavia. For some reason I missed out on hearing how the war started and what it was on about. None of the current news tells me this information. As a result I feel awfully lost when people talk about Bosnia-Herzegovina, Croats, Serbs, and the like. What I need is some background briefing in order to put the news into context. I need to know historical background, reasons for the conflict, who's on whose side.

What I need is something like I found recently while I was travelling on a plane. Being economically illiterate, I have always felt bamboozled by the morning news and its comments on the latest balance of payments or the deficit or any of those other catch-all phrases used by politicians and economists to describe the state of our nation's finances. However, while I browsed through one of the in-flight magazines I found something I'd always wanted—a one-page explanation of all the difficult terms used, in down to earth language that I could understand. Finally, I had some background briefing that enabled me to understand what was being said on the news and therefore helped me better to understand a very important part of my own country's situation.

---

example

Lets take a look at the book of Jonah to see if geography is helpful. There are a number of places mentioned in the book. Two important ones are Tarshish and Nineveh.

The first place to go for information on each of these places is the Bible itself. The references in the Psalms and the prophets (e.g. Ps 48:7; 72:10; Isa 23:6; 60:9) speak of Tarshish as a place of great ships. It is a somewhat distant and exotic place full of merchants and of goods (such as silver, iron, tin, and lead) that were in demand by the nations of the world (e.g. Ps 72:10; Isa 60:9; Jer 10:9; Ezek 27:12, 25). Isaiah 66:19 tells us that Tarshish is some distant place which has "not heard of the Lord's fame or seen his glory". This helps us understand what Jonah is doing when he "flees from the presence of the Lord". He is going as far as he can from God—that is, to Tarshish.

The city of Nineveh is mentioned 21 times in the NIV. Nine of those references concern the story of Jonah (seven in the book itself and two in the New Testament—Matt 12:41 and Lk 11:32). Seven occur in the book of Nahum. The first reference in the Bible, Genesis 10:11-12, is to the building of Nineveh in Assyria where it is called, as in Jonah, "the great city". The only other references are recorded in the parallel stories of Sennacherib's besieging of Jerusalem in 2 Kings 19 and Isaiah 36-37.

Step 3 is all about this process. It is about how we can find out background information that will help us understand what is being said when we read the Bible. It covers three important areas of background information: Geography, History and Word Meanings.

Step 3.1: Geography

The importance of geography

I remember the last time it happened. I was driving north through the city without a map, avoiding the main roads and hopefully the traffic. Right here. Left there. A one-way street and a couple of S bends negotiated.

I prided myself on my sense of direction. I could not admit defeat. Five minutes turned to twenty. I was completely lost. I admitted defeat.

I dived into the glove box, retrieved the street directory, looked for the nearest street sign and guessed at the suburb. As I found the street clearly marked on the map my whole mind did a

---

A word search on 'Assyria' would yield many more references scattered throughout the Old Testament. However, given the multitude of references it seems better to narrow them down a bit. A manageable way ahead would seem to be to look at the references in Jonah, read the Bible dictionary articles on 'Nineveh' and 'Assyria', and to look at a map to see its location. The references in Nahum might be helpful later as they appear to talk about Nineveh as it was about 100 years or so after the time of Jonah.

The *New Bible Dictionary* article on 'Nineveh' tells us that it was a principal city of the Assyrian country and became its last capital city. It was situated on the river Tigris in what is now Northern Iraq. In reference to its size the article says:

At the height of its prosperity Nineveh was enclosed by an inner wall of c. 12 km circuit within which, according to Felix Jones' survey of 1834, more than 175,000 persons could have lived. The population of "this great city" of Jonah's history (1:2; 3:2) is given as 120,000, who did not know right from wrong...The 'three days' journey may not necessarily designate the size of Nineveh (Jonah 3:3) whether by its circumference or total administrative district. It could refer to a day's journey in from the suburbs (cf. 3:4), a day for business and then return.

Finally, the references in Jonah itself tell us

180 degree turn. Somehow I had crossed back across Parramatta Road and was facing south again.

Looking at a map can do the same for your study of the Bible. It can turn your mind around the right way. You can see where you are and where you are going. Reading a map can help you to understand your Bible.

The truth is that geography can be important for biblical inter-pretation and that many parts of the Bible will remain closed to us unless we understand the fundamentals of the geography of the Ancient Near East, and Palestine in particular. Climate and geo-graphical circumstances often influence the thought, language and idiom of a writer, and leave an imprint on his literary productions.

If you would like a 'bird's-eye' view or summary of the impor-tant geographical areas in the study of the Bible, you might like to read through the Appendix on 'An Overview of Biblical Geography'. Although there are many good Bible atlases, the most helpful book for me (apart from the maps in the back of my Bible) has been the *Bible Mapbook* by Simon Jenkins (Herts: Lion, 1985).

---

example

that Nineveh was a large and important city in the world in which Jonah lived (1:2; 3:2-3; 4:11). It was a city known by God because of its wickedness (not unlike Sodom and Gomorrah and the surrounding cities mentioned in Genesis 18-19).

It needs to be said at this point that, if we knew nothing more about Nineveh than these references in Jonah, we should still have no trouble understanding the book. If you are finding all of this research rather daunting, don't fret. Jonah still makes sense to those of us who aren't geographers.

Step 3.2: History

Some basic assumptions

There are some basic assumptions that need to be acknowledged as we interpret the Bible:

- The Word of God originated in an historical setting. Knowing something of the history may therefore help us understand it better.
- The place, time and circumstances of an author and the prevailing view of the world naturally will colour his writings.

These assumptions have implications for us, as readers in the twentieth century. We will benefit from:

- Getting to know the biblical author. Where is he as he writes? What things have influenced his life? What things influence him now? What is he like as a person? What was his purpose in writing? Are there any special circumstances behind the writing of this book/letter?
- Getting to know the original readers. Where are they as they receive this letter? Why are they there? What has influenced them in the past or is influencing them at present?
- Getting to know the historical circumstances. What political powers are there? What is the state of the nation to which the readers belong? What religious habits and institutions are there?

The author

The first question to ask of any piece of literature is: who is the author?

Some of the books of the Bible let us know; some don't. However, when the author is named it is often because it is important. In these cases, we need to become acquainted with him. The best way to do this is to become familiar with his writings, paying attention to personal touches and incidental remarks that bear on his character and life.

A variation on this question is to ask, 'Who is the speaker?' The Bible often records the words of people other than the writer and it is important to recognise this and distinguish between them. Most instances are easy to pick up (e.g. in narrative); others are not so easy (e.g. Jn 3:16-21; Gal 2). In the prophets it is quite common for the prophet to switch back and forth between the human author and divine speech. This transition can usually be picked up by noticing changes from the third to first persons. Sometimes, the author quotes other people (e.g. supposed opponents in Mal 3:13-16; Rom 3:1-9; 1 Cor).

The recipients

If we are to understand a particular piece of literature we will often need to try and work out what it might have meant to the original readers/hearers. Becoming acquainted with the original recipients is especially important with the prophetic books and the New Testament letters (and less important with wisdom books and the Gospels). Almost all of these books were directed to very special circumstances and to particular needs. The author often took into account geographical, historical, social, industrial, political and commercial situations in framing his message. He often took advantage of his readers' moral and religious character, their personal idiosyncrasies, their prejudices and peculiar habits of thought. Knowing the original hearers often makes a difference between understanding or not understanding a particular passage.

When we looked at 'the author' we noted that there was sometimes a need to be aware of an extra category of 'speakers'. We should also look out for 'hearers' who are not the people to whom the literature is directed but people within the text who hear a particular person speak (e.g. the Israelites listening to Moses).

The contemporary situation

There are some parts of the Bible that cannot be pinned down in terms of time or space. They are, in some sense, timeless. However, much of the Bible is closely tied to an historical situation. The national history of Israel, its political institutions, its alliances, its relationships with other nations, and its kings and leaders, all play an important part in what the author is conveying to his readers.

The God of the Bible is the Lord of history. As the Lord of history, he comes to his people as they dwell in real historical situations and speaks to them there. If we are to understand what he is saying to them and how they are meant to react, we will need to acquaint ourselves with their situation and the various forces at work. For example, the words of Psalm 137–"Blessed is he who takes your children and smashes their heads against a rock"–will be difficult to understand unless we are acquainted with the people of Israel in Babylon, their circumstances there, and the factors that brought them there.

Practically speaking

So what do we do? What sort of questions do we need to ask? Where can we get the information?

The author

- Go back to the beginning of the book. Read it through again. As you do, note down everything the author tells you about himself.
- For example, note down his name, his job, his feelings, his credentials, his situation now, his biases, his attitudes to his hearers, the sort of allusions/illustrations he uses, and so on.
- Get out your concordance and see if he is referred to anywhere else in Scripture. But beware–if you find the same name, don't automatically assume that it's the same person!
- If your author has written anything else, have a go at reading it and ask yourself the same sorts of questions as above (about the author's character, situation, etc.).
- Ask yourself if any of the things you have found out about your author seem to have influenced what he is saying in the passage you are looking at.
- Check out his name in a Bible dictionary. See what it has to say about him.

The recipients

- Again, go back to the beginning of the book. Read it through again. Note down everything it tells you (either directly or by inference) about the original readers. For example, ask yourself: What is their situation? Are they involved in behaviour that needs correcting? Are they in need of rebuke, encouragement, praise, exhortation or teaching? Is their problem a moral or theological one? If there is a theological problem, has the teaching come from outside or inside the group of people? What does the author know of their situation? How did he come to know?
- Think about the rest of the Bible. Do other parts of the Bible give you some important historical background to the people, relationships or situations addressed here?
- Ask yourself about the relationship between the author and the recipients. Does the relationship have any impact on how they have received, are receiving, or will receive the things he says?

example

The book of Jonah has no stated author (although Jonah is presented as the author of Jonah 2 at least, and his personal history as told in Jonah 1 is of obvious importance in understanding the psalm of Jonah 2). Moreover, there are no stated original readers either. Therefore, our only concern under this Step is to look at the contemporary history as implied by the book.

But before we have a look at the contemporary history it is probably important to make some observations regarding Jonah and the problem of authorship and original readers. A number of commentators proceed in the following manner:

- *They do the careful reading of the text of Jonah.*

- *They observe that the Gentile response to God's word, and God's favourable response to them, seems important.*
- *They imagine an historical context that might have given rise to such an emphasis.*
- *They then read back this purpose into the book and suggest an original author or group of authors and an original readership and a date or historical time that might have given rise to this emphasis.*
- *They then read the text in the light of this reconstruction.*

The end results are highly speculative and have no certainty behind them. It is probably better to understand that if God has given this book to us

- Check out a Bible Dictionary. What does it have to say about the original recipients?

The contemporary situation

- Get out your concordance and find out anything you can about the people mentioned in the text, the political powers at the time, the religious institutions mentioned, and so on.
- Look up relevant articles in a Bible dictionary or the introduction to a good commentary and repeat the exercise. If you have the time and inclination (and a good library nearby), pursue some of these matters further from the bibliography provided at the end of the dictionary article.
- Having done all this, jot down some of your thoughts as to why the author wrote this section within the book you are reading.

---

without a particular author and situation being explicitly stated, then we ought to interpret it in this manner and see its principles as being universal and timeless.

Having said this, let's have a look at the contemporary situation of the book. There are two references which tie the book down historically. The first is the reference to Jonah (2 Kings 14:25) and the second is the reference to Nineveh (Jon 1:1-2).

2 Kings 14:23-28

23 In the fifteenth year of Amaziah son of Joash king of Judah, Jeroboam son of Jehoash king of Israel became king in Samaria, and he reigned forty-one years. 24 He did evil in the eyes of the Lord and did not turn away from any of the sins of Jeroboam son of Nebat, which he had caused Israel to commit. 25 He was the one who restored the boundaries of Israel from Lebo Hamath to the Sea of the Arabah, in accordance with the word of the Lord, the God of Israel, spoken through his servant Jonah son of Amittai, the prophet from Gath Hepher.

26 The Lord had seen how bitterly everyone in Israel, whether slave or free, was suffering; there was no one to help them. 27 And since the Lord had not said he would blot out the name of Israel from under heaven, he saved them by the hand of Jeroboam son of Jehoash.

28 As for the other events of Jeroboams reign, all he did, and his military achievements, including how he

Aids in determining the import of the historical situation

- The best resource you can bring to the study of the historical situation of the Bible, is a good grasp of the whole Bible. The Bible itself is the principal resource for knowing the history of the life and times of biblical people. Get into the habit of reading large slabs of the Bible in an easy to read version of the Bible (e.g. New International Version or Good News Bible).
- There are also a number of good, short histories of the Bible that are well worth reading. Get hold of one of these for a bird's-eye view of the flow of biblical history.
- A very helpful book on understanding the ancient world is John Thompson's *Handbook of Life in Bible Times* (IVP, 1986).

---

example

recovered for Israel both Damascus and Hamath, which had belonged to Yaudi, are they not written in the book of the annals of the kings of Israel? (NIV) It seems most likely that the two references (2 Kgs 14:25 & Jon 1:1) are to the same Jonah, son of Amittai. Therefore, while the book of Jonah doesn't say when the events recorded actually occurred, we can take a good guess that they took place during the reign of Jeroboam II (i.e. approximately 782-753 BC).

The Bible dictionaries tell us that the reigns of Ashurnasirpal II (883-859 BC) and Shalmaneser III (859-824 BC) were marked by a period of remarkable growth and prosperity for Assyria. The end of the reign of Shalmaneser III began a period of significant decline that did not end until the reign of Tiglath Pileser III (745-727 BC). The records from the Assyrians themselves tell us that there were two events that occurred that were viewed as particularly ominous: a famine (perhaps from 765 to 759 BC) and a solar eclipse on 15 June 763.

As one commentator has suggested, had Jonah appeared in Nineveh about this time, his message might well have drawn the kind of response that is recorded in chapter 3 of the book of Jonah.

hands on

1. Think about the geography and history of the place in which you live. How do these things affect the lifestyle, values, and culture of that place?

2. a. In the space below write down an explanation of either (i) how you became a Christian, or (ii) how you came to be engaged in your current occupation.

   b. Does your explanation include references to historical factors that influenced your decision (e.g. your personal situation at the time, your upbringing, etc.)? Could you answer these questions without referring to historical factors?

Step 3.1: Geography

3. Crete and Nicopolis are both mentioned in the book of Titus. Find out where Crete is on a map and put together a description of it and its people from the following sources: the book of Acts (chapter 27); the book of Titus; and the *New Bible Dictionary* article on 'Crete'.
   Find out what you can about 'Nicopolis'.

hands on

Step 3.2: History

4. Find out what you can about Paul's location as he writes and his personal situation. What is his relationship with Titus?

5. Find out what you can about Titus. The New Testament references are in 2 Corinthians 2:13; 2 Corinthians 7-8; Galatians 2:1-3; 2 Timothy 4:10. Compare what you find with the article on him in a Bible dictionary.

6. What do you learn about the situation in the church/es in Crete from the letter itself?

רחוב הַיְּהוּדִים

طريق حارة اليهود

JEWISH QUARTER RD.

...y wind of Melbourne
cut through me like cold steel.
As I waited for the train,
I browsed the new wave
graffiti that covered every
inch of the freshly painted
ticket box.

PTO

STEP
4

Word
meanings

THE ICY WIND of Melbourne cut through me like cold steel. As I waited for the train, I browsed the new wave graffiti that covered every inch of the freshly painted ticket box—a symbol of an endless battle for supremacy.

But wait...there! In the middle of that sentence. A word not met. A new word, not yet defined in my Macquarie Dictionary. A word fresh from the fevered imagination of some fifteen-year-old, with nothing to do and nowhere to go in the early hours of yet another day.

All day that word bothered me. What did it mean? Where could I go to find out?

If you wanted to find out the meaning of a new word you had just discovered on a ticket office door in some inner city suburb of Melbourne, what would you do? Where would you go to find out?

Probably your first thought would be to find out the meaning from the context of the sentence. Does it appear to be a verb or a noun? A second option would be to hide somewhere on the train station at 3.00 am, capture this anonymous fifteen-year-old graffitist and ask for the meaning. Presuming this was inconvenient, perhaps you could browse other walls on the station, attempting to find other occurrences of its use.

Another option would be to find a group of people that he/she spends time with. You could wander through the neighbourhood looking for the sorts of people that might be likely to spend their idle moments inscribing their initials and messages on train ticket offices. Upon finding such people, you could ask them if they had any idea as to the meaning of the word.

You could also ask people in general who live in the neighbourhood. Maybe they have heard the word in use somewhere and know its meaning? Moving further afield, you could ask the people you were staying with in another suburb of Melbourne, even if they don't frequent railway stations in the early hours of the morning. There is, however, a diminishing chance of coming up with a promising meaning using this course of action.

It makes sense, doesn't it? The meaning of a particular word is most clearly determined by the context in which it originally occurred. As you move out in concentric circles to more distant people and places, the possibility of finding meaning is also more distant. Meaning is best determined by its most immediate context.

It is like this with the Bible. If you are reading a passage of the Bible and come across a word you don't understand, then the way to determine its meaning is to start with the most immediate context and work outwards, placing the most stress upon the most immediate context.

The meaning of words

What sort of words am I looking for?

When we read our Bibles we come across two sorts of words that need clarification:

- words which are completely new to us (e.g. 'propitiation', 'gleanings', 'behemoth').
- words which we have encountered before and which already have some meaning because of our prior knowledge (e.g. 'grace', 'judgement', 'love', 'peace').

The words in this second category require clarification for a number of reasons. They may be significant because they are theologically loaded (e.g. 'hope', 'righteousness'), or because they clearly make a difference to the meaning of the passage (e.g. 'body' in 1 Thess 4:4). They might be important because they are catch words which are repeated through the passage (e.g. 'boast' in 2 Cor 10-12). Sometimes, words which would normally be insignificant become very significant because of their context in the passage you are looking at (e.g. the word 'work' as a technical term for Paul's ministry).

What do I do when I have found them?

The procedure for dealing with both sorts of words is similar, although new words need some additional information.

Establish a broad range of meaning

When you come across a new word you should firstly establish a broad range of meaning for it, that is, a range of the possible senses that the word might have. This can be done using a dictionary (Hebrew, Greek, or even English). This gives you a starting point for determining its meaning in the context of the passage. You need to be aware, however, that this is only a starting point. A dictionary meaning only gets you up and running. It doesn't help much more than this.

For example, suppose I were new to Australia and I read the word 'kettle' somewhere. I could go and look up the Macquarie Dictionary and it would establish a broad range of meaning for me. For example, it would tell me that a kettle was "a portable container with a cover, a spout, and a handle, in which to boil water for making tea and other uses", or "an open vessel for heating metals of low melting point" or an abbreviation for a 'kettledrum' or even part of a colloquial saying—'a kettle of fish'—which means "a mess, muddle, or awkward state of affairs".

Hence, to determine the meaning of the word 'kettle' in a particular context I'm going to have to do some more work by looking at the context. So, I could find that the word 'kettle' is preceded by the words "she hit the..." Even this could mean a number of things, depending on whether the person who was doing the hitting of the kettle was in the kitchen or in an orchestra. The point is that we must place stress on the meaning that comes from the immediate context, not from the dictionary. We must be ready to sacrifice the meaning we have brought from outside if the most immediate context demands it.

- Look at the passage in which the word appears and see if the context helps determine the meaning.
- Look to see if the word is used elsewhere in the same docu-

ment and what it means there.

- Look at other writings by the same person to see how they use the word there.
- Look at what the word means to other people writing at the same time, from different backgrounds.
- Look at what the word means to other people writing at the same time from similar backgrounds and under similar influences. For example, Peter and Paul are writing at the same time. They are both Jews influenced by the Old Testament. They are both Christians, influenced by the teachings of Jesus.
- Consider the writings/teachings of other people whose words or teaching have significantly influenced the author. For example, the teaching of Jesus, recorded for us in the Gospels obviously exerts a powerful influence on the authors of the rest of the New Testament, especially in the area of theological words and ethical application.

Remember not to restrict your work to the same part of speech. If you are looking at a noun in your passage, don't forget to chase up the verb or adjective with the same meaning. For example, if you are looking at what Paul means by faith, also look at how he uses the words 'faithfulness' and 'to believe'.

If you have done all this, your 'range of meaning' will probably have undergone a shift. It may have become broader, or it may have tightened up considerably. Now that your range of meaning has sharpened up and the background to the use of your word has become a bit clearer, go back and look at the word in its context. Do your first tentative conclusions still stand? What meaning now makes most sense here? Remember the aim of this exercise: to find the meaning of *this word* in *this context*.

Notice that we only suggest looking up the Old Testament when trying to find the meaning of a New Testament word. The reason is obvious: the New Testament could not have influenced the use of the word in the Old Testament. Influence can only flow from older sources to newer ones and not vice versa.

Things to remember

Remember that the immediate context is the most important factor in determining the meaning of a passage

A word can have a unique meaning in its context. Just because it is never used in a particular way anywhere else in the Bible, doesn't mean that it can't mean that here. Language is not based on statistics, but on usage. Words function in a context, not on their own.

Remember not to go overboard in analyzing a word

Don't make too much of specific words in a particular context. Like us, the authors of the Bible did not always choose their words as carefully as our analysis seems to presuppose. There is often a better reason for why an author used a word than its bare meaning. It might have sounded better, or fitted better with the other words in the sentence, or rhymed, or have been a synonym for another word.

Don't forget grammar

In ordinary circumstances we don't utter isolated words or phrases, but whole sentences. Remember that although every sentence must be composed of words, not every string of words is a sentence. Knowing the meaning of individual words is no guarantee that you know what the sentence means. The meaning of a sentence is dependent upon how those words are strung together.

Aids for finding meanings

Bible dictionaries and encyclopedias

Bible dictionaries and encyclopedias are a veritable mine of biblical information (and trivia!). They are usually alphabetically arranged and contain articles treating important biblical ideas, books, words, people and concepts. They are designed to give a general grasp of the issues involved. They also give an extended bibliography for those interested in doing further reading.

A good basic dictionary is the *Lion Handbook to the Bible*. A bit more technical and fuller is *The New Bible Dictionary* or its illustrated, three volume equivalent *The Illustrated Bible Dictionary*. (There is also a concise version of *The New Bible Dictionary* available). I would class a *New Bible Dictionary* as an essential tool for systematic, informed Bible study.

Biblical wordbooks and lexicons

At another level there are biblical wordbooks and lexicons. These convey much more specific, detailed information about what words mean by looking at their usage in the Old and New Testaments and in the literature of the time.

There are a number of such wordbooks for those using English translations. A good one, although a little technical, is *The New International Dictionary of New Testament Theology*.

Biblical concordances

A biblical concordance is a necessity for doing the sort of things advocated in this Step. In the hands of someone who is used to it, a concordance is a sophisticated and invaluable tool. It enables the user to trace how a word is used throughout the Bible. Almost all established translations of the Bible now have an extensive concordance readily available.

Cross reference Bibles

Another helpful aid in interpreting the Bible is a good cross reference Bible. A cross reference Bible takes key words or ideas in the passage you are reading and gives cross references to other passages where the same word or idea is used. Cross references will also point to parallel passages, or passages which may have influenced the thought of the writer at this point. An experienced user of a cross reference Bible can look up a whole chain of related passages or ideas through the use of the cross references. The best cross reference Bibles are those which have been compiled by a group of people rather than an individual, as the latter may be influenced by the prejudices of the compiler.

English dictionaries

While an English dictionary may be useful for establishing an initial temporary meaning, we need to be careful. The words in the Bible are Hebrew and Greek words which have been translated into English. Many of the terms are part of a technical vocabulary (e.g. 'covenant', 'repentance') and definitions of such terms in standard English dictionaries will be adequate only at the most basic level.

A basic library

I would suggest the following as a basic library for someone wanting to study the Bible well:

- A good general reading Bible (e.g. NIV).
- A more literal word-for-word translation of the Bible (e.g. RV, RSV, NASB, NRSV) with cross references.
- An extensive concordance for use with your more literal translation.
- A *New Bible Dictionary.*

These days some good computer programs supply you with most or all of these, plus a bit more. If you have access to the technology, this might be the way to go.

Mistakes to avoid

Overusing a cross reference Bible or computer word searches

Some time ago I came across this little poem called "Why are fire engines red?"

> *Why are fire engines red?*
> *They have four wheels and eight men;*
> *four plus eight is twelve;*
> *twelve inches make a ruler;*
> *a ruler is Queen Elizabeth;*

Queen Elizabeth sails the seven seas;
the seven seas have fish;
the fish have fins;
the Finns hate the Russians;
the Russians are red;
fire engines are always rushin';
so they're red.

As we read the poem we recognise it for what it is—an intricate but ridiculous play on words and their associations. And yet I have seen people do similar things with cross reference Bibles. They start with one word and pursue connections through the cross references and end up with an intricate but highly dubious theological conclusion. Alternatively, they end up proving a correct theological point by highly dubious means. Be careful with word associations. Keep to the rules suggested above.

Deriving word meanings from etymology

Etymology is the study of the history of particular words and their derivation. Some word books (especially those designed for preachers.) are prone to explaining the meaning of a word by looking at how it came into existence. Often this means looking at its component words. Hence the word for 'church' in Greek is *ekklesia*. Students of the Bible have noticed that this word is derived from two Greek words *ek* and *kaleo* which, when combined mean 'to call out'. They have then said that the meaning of *ekklesia* is 'to call out' and made much mileage out of the fact that the church is God's 'called out' people. However, although the root words are indeed as suggested, this meaning is simply never within the range of meanings of the word in New Testament times.

Overusing dictionaries

We need to be wary of using dictionaries too rigorously in determining what a word means. This is true whether the dictionary is a simple English dictionary or one on the Hebrew or Greek. An example on each might help.

The first example is of the word 'worship' and illustrates both the unhelpful use of etymology (see above) and the unhelpful use of English dictionaries. Our modern word 'worship' is derived from the English word *worthscip* or *weorthscipe* which is

example

In the book of Jonah there is a series of words describing God that appear to belong together. In the NIV they are: 'grace' (2:8); 'compassion' (3:9, 10; 4:2); 'gracious' (4:2); and 'love' (4:2). Since these words seem to cover a similar broad range of meanings, I thought I would try and see if any of them are actually the same words in the original and try and narrow down the meanings. I thought I'd start by looking at some other translations. The results of my search are set out in the table below.

My examination of the translations only helped me a little in the following three areas:

• *It appeared to indicate that the NIV has added the word compassion in 3:9-10. where no other word*

occurs (unless all the other translations have omitted it).
• *All translations translate the NIV's gracious the same way in 4:2.*
• *All translations have words relating to love for the third word describing God's character in 4:2. As a result, we can't really tell whether the words used here are similar or linked in any way.*

The best way ahead seems to be to put aside the references in chapter 3 and concentrate on the three words in chapter 4 which the NIV translates as 'gracious', 'compassionate' and 'love'.

The context helps us with their meaning to some extent. Being gracious and compassionate, slow to

Reference	NIV	RSV	NASB	NRSV
2.8	grace	true loyalty	faithfulness	true loyalty
3.9	compassion	[doesn't occur]	[doesn't occur]	[doesn't occur]
3.10	compassion	[doesn't occur]	[doesn't occur]	[doesn't occur]
4.2	gracious	gracious	gracious	gracious
4.2	compassionate	merciful	compassionate	merciful
4.2	love	steadfast love	lovingkindness	steadfast love

made up of two words, *weorth* (our word 'worth') and the ending *-scipe* which was used as suffix on nouns to denote state, character, condition, office, skill, etc. Hence 'worship' can mean the state of being of worth, or perhaps even (as many have noted) the attributing of worth. Hence, worship is attributing supreme worth to God, whose character is of extreme worth.

Now while the sentiment is laudable, the definition is far from being biblical and yet it has so infiltrated our thinking that even the Bible's own teaching is pushed aside in the favour of it.

---

anger and abounding in love, is linked with relenting or turning back from sending calamity and with being concerned (4:11). We know what this is like from chapter 3 where we see God turning back from judgement when people repent. It is also set against the sort of attitude that Jonah has of storing up his anger and remaining unforgiving (ch 4).

The cross references to 4:2 lead to Exodus 34:6, where God gives Moses the definitive revelation of who he is and what he is like. He is "The Lord, the Lord, the compassionate and gracious God, slow to anger, abounding in love and faithfulness, maintaining love to thousands, and forgiving wickedness, rebellion and sin. Yet he does not leave the guilty unpunished; he punishes the children and their children for the sin of the fathers to the third and fourth generation." This statement comes in the context of God having relented of his intention to destroy Israel in Exodus 32.

However, my cross reference Bible also points me beyond Exodus 34. I find that there are similar quotes in Psalm 103:8ff and Joel 2:12-14. Joel 2:12-14 and the surrounding verses look particularly apt, given the book of Jonah:

"Even now," declares the Lord,
"return to me with all your heart,
with fasting and weeping and mourning."
Rend your heart
and not your garments.
Return to the Lord your God,
for he is gracious and compassionate,
slow to anger and abounding in love,
and he relents from sending calamity.
Who knows? He may turn and have pity
and leave behind a blessing—
grain offerings and drink offerings
for the Lord your God.

Having done this groundwork in the Bible itself, without outside help, perhaps it is time to see what some of the Bible dictionaries and wordbooks say. To start off, I chased the words 'love' and 'grace'. In one way, these books didn't help all that much because I was looking for a word or group of words that obviously can be translated in a variety of ways and don't have just one English equivalent. In another way, these books helped because they showed I was on the right track.

The second example is contained within the many common word books or dictionaries of biblical literature themselves. Many of these books give you much more than just the range of meaning like our English dictionaries. Rather, they are more like encyclopedias, giving us masses of information that covers a much broader period than we are probably studying.

Thinking that particular words are always packed with theological meaning

Often common words can be theologically 'loaded' in other contexts. Hence, the word 'love' (Greek *agape*) which is often theologically loaded with the idea of sacrificial self-giving, appears to have few of these connotations in Luke 11:43 ("Woe to you Pharisees, because you love the most important seats in the synagogues...").

Assuming that word meanings are always static across all a writer's works

This book is actually a substantial revision of a previous book I wrote. As I've written it, I've made plenty of changes. Some of these changes have come about because I have changed some of my thinking on some issues. Other changes are more cosmetic, that is, words I once used now mean something quite different to me. In other words, the meaning of certain words I used six years ago has undergone a change. This is an experience common to all of us. So the word 'gay' now means something quite different from what it meant to us thirty years ago.

Because of this we need to make sure that we don't automatically assume that a word used by Paul in one of this letters must automatically mean the same thing in another of his letters. For example, the word 'church' in Paul's earlier letters seems to almost exclusively refer to a local gathering of Christians (e.g. 1 Thess 1:1) while his later letters use it also to refer to a more heavenly or spiritual gathering to which Christians all over the world belong (e.g. Col 1:18).

hands on

1. Read Philippians 4:7 in its context. Outline the steps you would take in working out what the word 'peace' means here.

Step 3.3: Word meanings

2. Go through your text of Titus 2 writing down the words which:
    a. you don't understand; and

    b. which appear to be significant.

hands on

3. Where relevant, go through the steps for discovering the meaning of the words you noted down. Use a concordance, cross reference Bible and Bible dictionary where necessary. (I've listed some of the words from chapter 2 which I think might be important and have left some space for you to summarise your findings about each of them).

sound doctrine

subject

self-controlled

grace

godly/ungodliness

saviour

temperate

seriousness

In this section we sum up what we have done so far before we try to understand how a Bible passage fits into the larger biblical picture and how it affects our lives.

PTO

STEP
5

Sum up your progress

IN THIS SECTION we sum up what we have done so far before we try to understand how a Bible passage fits into the larger biblical picture and how it affects our lives. There are two steps in the process. First, we put the passage into its context. Second, we try to imagine what impact the passage would have had on the original readers.

Step 5.1: Context

Poems (and the same could be said of novels, short stories and even essays) are like elaborate, well-structured buildings: they have an overall unity composed of many substructures. But skyscrapers do not exist in isolation. The Sears building in Chicago does not rise up out of nowhere and exist in relation to nothing. Much shorter buildings surround it, and buildings almost as tall peer across the city-scape, slowly turning various shades of gray and brown and green. To understand the function of the Sears skyscraper, we must see not only its internal structure but its place in the city—one city, Chicago—in its relation to commerce, to the arts, to the ongoing life of the city. And then we must see it as one dot in an even larger picture—the economy, the architecture, the life of the country. There is no end, this side of the stars, to the links this building has to life at large. It would be no exaggeration to say that in order to understand the Sears building we would have to understand the universe. And then, of course, we hasten to say, we can't do that.

James Sire, *The Joy of Reading*

Our studies started off with us reading the whole of a book—the big picture. Before too long, we got into the nitty gritty of one particular passage within the book—the little picture. Now it's time to return to the big picture. We need to stand back and ask ourselves how this particular 'little picture' fits into the whole. In so doing, we are recognising that the passage we are studying is part of a larger whole. We want to avoid the pitfall of 'atomising' the book we are studying–of not seeing the forest for the trees.

Our aim is to see how all the parts fit together into a whole, and how to relate the piece we are studying to what went before and what comes after.

There are two steps to this:

- Find the overarching purpose of the book we are reading.
- Work out how each part serves that overarching purpose.

Establishing the purpose of a book

Sometimes this is easy, in that the author states his purpose explicitly (e.g. Lk 1:1-4). However, most of the time, the author is not so obliging. Either way, we will need to read the whole section or book again (the notes you made in 'Step 2.1 Getting acquainted' may help!). Ask yourself: Does the author explicitly state his purpose in writing? Does he imply a purpose? What are the special emphases or concerns that emerge? What words or ideas are frequently repeated? What, if anything, do these tell you about the purpose of the book?

When you are reading through the book, keep in mind that the author often gives away his purpose either explicitly or implicitly at the beginning or end of the book.

The question of context

There are two aspects of context that need to be looked at: literary context and ideological context.

Literary context

Here we are trying to find out how the overall structure of the book fits together as a *literary* unit and how it flows.

We need to ask these sort of questions: Is the passage self-contained? What is the point of this passage? How does it fit with what came before and what comes after? How does it fit into the overall book? Why was it included at this particular place?

As you do this, pay particular attention to the use of conjunctions (e.g. 'and', 'therefore', 'but').

Ideological context

In this aspect, we are trying to find out how the overall ideas (as in 'idea-ology') fit together and flow. As well as repeating some of

---

example

In this example, I have another look at the book of Jonah to see if I can draw together some of the threads of my work so far. First, I look to see if the purpose of the book can be established or glimpsed from a surface reading. Second, I look at the literary and ideological context to see if they support or help in establishing the purpose.

Establishing the purpose

When I read the book again, I found that a number of things that had not been clear to me on first reading now made sense, thanks to my detailed work on each of the chapters. They can be summarised along the following lines:

• *There is no explicitly stated purpose in writing. On the surface it appears simply as a story of God's relationship with a recalcitrant prophet.*
• *There are a number of special emphases or concerns that emerge as you read the story.*
• *The word of God: The book is framed around the two statements: "the word of the LORD came to Jonah" in Jonah 1:1 and 3:1. Each of the sections*

introduced by these phrases also ends with a word from God: "Then the LORD spoke (2:10); "Then the LORD said" (4:10).
• *God's control (sovereignty): The passages seem to pick up on God's sovereign actions. He controls all things and does what he pleases with the world.*
• *The attitude of pagans and of Jonah to God's purpose: There is a constant contrast between pagans who are willing to embrace God's purpose and Jonah's reluctance concerning it.*

All of these elements are clear in the surface reading of the book. However, my detailed study has revealed some more threads which help tie things together for me.

The question of context

Literary context

I decided to go back over the major parts of Jonah to see how they fit together. I thought this might give me a stronger indication as to why the author wrote the book. Although I've given you my work in chapter 1 earlier, here's what I thought of the book as a whole.

the questions we asked about literary context, we need to ask: What is the point that the author is making in this passage? Why is this particular passage included in the whole? How does it serve the overall purpose of the author?

Up until now, most of our questions have been 'what' questions (e.g. What genre? What meaning? What geographical/ historical context?). Now we are asking the 'how' and 'why' questions. Having done all this, the inevitable next step is to put it all together. This is the purpose of the final part of 'Step 5: Summing up your progress'.

---

chapter 1: The focus is on 'fear'. We are told that Jonah 'fears' or 'worships God' but his fear seems fairly flimsy when contrasted with the fear of the sailors. In other words, the idea of fear is a way of showing up the sailors in a positive light compared to Jonah.

chapter 2: This chapter has obvious literary similarities with chapter 1. Jonah goes through a similar experience to the sailors. Like the sailors:

• *Jonah faces a crisis (peril from the sea);*
• *cries to the Lord and acknowledges God's control over the world;*
• *is saved by God, and*
• *offers praise and thanksgiving.*

Why would the writer structure things this way?

Perhaps he wants us to focus on the fact that God is generous to both Jews *and* Gentiles. Salvation comes from the Lord (for both Jews and Gentiles) — Jonah 2:9.

chapter 3: The general structure of chapters 1 and 2 is again picked up in chapter 3. Again God judges (in the prophecy of doom). Again there is repentance and again there is rescue or deliverance.

If this analysis is right then perhaps this repetitive structure is deliberately there to prepare us for chapter 4. Jonah has seen God repeatedly as one who is gracious and kind, not wanting any to perish but all to come to repentance. He knew this in theory from Exodus 34. He knew it in experience from his own encounter with the fish. Moreover, he tells us that it was because he knew this of God that he had fled to Tarshish in the first.

chapter 4: The book closes with a dialogue between Jonah and God over the rightness or otherwise of Jonah's anger. The content and the structure is such that we find ourselves asking, "Will Jonah repent this time? Will he accept that God is generous and that his own fate, that of his people, and that of the world is dependent on him being able to exercise his spontaneous and often unexpected grace and mercy?"

Ideological context

If we ask ourselves, "What is the dominant idea throughout the book?", the answer seems clear from the quotation of Exodus 34 in chapter 4 and the allusion to it in 1:8 and 3:9-10. The God of Jonah is the God revealed to Moses, that is, he is Yahweh, the gracious and merciful God, slow to anger, abounding in steadfast love, and ready to relent from punishing.

The book appears to function as an explanation of the implications of this statement. In its original context it clearly had his special people in mind. The book of Jonah appears to be saying that we can't restrict God's revelation to his people. His love is spontaneous and unexpected, which means it could easily and appropriately be expressed to those outside the covenant people.

Step 5.2: Summing up

I stood beside what remained of my mother's car and stared back down the road, past the swirl of black skid marks, towards the other vehicle. It was pushed into the rock face at the side of the road and even in the darkness I could make out two unconscious—but fortunately still alive—figures slumped over the dashboard. While my legs rushed towards them the rest of me fled, not wanting to see, not wanting to face reality.

But reality had to be faced. I was guilty. I was responsible. I knew it; they knew it; and the policemen who took the report knew it, even as I lied to them. And as I faced this reality, I gradually began to ponder other things. I thought about the events that led to the accident. I pondered the way my life was heading. And, almost imperceptibly, my view of reality began to change. I began to reorder my view of the world and of myself in it. I reorganised my priorities. I determined that some previously important things to me were no longer important.

It was as though the impact of the accident had taken all the neat little files in my mind which represented my view of the world and had thrown them into the wind. As I scrambled to put them back, I realised that they could be put back differently and that I had been stupid to put them where I had in the first place. Six months later my whole view of the world, of reality, of God and of myself was totally reorganised. I realised that God had to be the centre of my life rather than me. I re-examined the words, deeds and claims of Jesus and recognised that it was only in him that I could find meaning, forgiveness and direction. Life could never be the same again.

In his book *The Joy of Reading,* James Sire takes up an idea put forward by Alvin Toffler that "Every person carries in his head a mental model of the world, a subjective representation of external reality". Sire likens this mental model to a giant filing cabinet in which we can file all the information that comes our way. He says that the major files in this filing cabinet include the following basic concepts:

- our concept of the most real thing in existence (our notion of God or of ultimate reality)
- our view of the essential nature of the external world (ordered or chaotic, material or spiritual)
- our idea of who we and others really are (our concept of human nature); this includes our idea of how we know things (epistemology) and our notion of the good (ethics)
- our understanding of the meaning of humanity's sojourn on earth (the meaning of history).

Recognising that we all have a view of the world and of reality is very helpful to us in biblical interpretation. It helps us understand ourselves and it helps us grasp what is going on in the Scriptures.

Our world view

Each of us comes to the Bible with our own presuppositions, world view or 'mental model' of the world. If we are Christians then we come to the Bible as people who have given our whole beings to God. Our desire in life is that we should "not be conformed to the world, but be transformed" (Rom 12:1-2). As Christians, we recognise that this happens through God changing the way we think. God transforms us through "the renewal of our minds, so that we may prove what is the will of God, what is good and acceptable and perfect."

When we read the Bible, then, we are doing some re-programming. We are allowing the God who caused the Bible to be written to target our current ungodly ways of viewing reality and change them so that they are more godly. We want God to change our ways of thinking, acting and feeling so that they are more in line with his will. We want his world view to be our world view, his wishes our command.

God's view

As Christians, we also believe that the biblical author is writing under the influence of the same God whose will we want to know and live by. We believe that, as he writes, he is not only conveying

---

example

Having done most of the detailed work on the book of Jonah, I'm now in a position to begin to ask what impact the passage might have had on the original readers. Inevitably, this has an element of speculation, although hopefully it is well informed speculation.

We have a small problem with Jonah in that we don't actually know the original readership. We don't know if they were people during Jonah's time or whether they were people of a much later time to whom the story of Jonah had particular relevance. However, given that the book is written in Hebrew and enclosed in Hebrew Scriptures, it is a reasonable assumption that it is directed to an original readership that is Jewish.

What does Jonah teach the original readers?

What we can work out with some degree of certainty is what it told the original readers of God, the world, themselves, and other people.

About God

As we noted in the previous step, the picture of God is a grand one. He is the Creator of all the world. He controls it and oversees every element of its working. He makes seas to storm and plants to grow and fish to swallow prophets. He is the Lord of heaven and earth, the maker of the sea and the dry land.

This Creator is also the God whose gracious and spontaneous love is surprisingly shown, not only toward Israel but also toward others. He is not a God whose love is selective. If his love is spontaneous and generous and surprising, then people should not be surprised if it is directed to those outside Israel.

About the world and the people in it

As for the world and the people in it, the book is clear that both Jews and Gentiles have problems before God. Ninevites may be renowned for their wickedness, but Jonah is famous for his disobedience and hard-heartedness. All are dependent on God's grace for rescue. Furthermore, all are the recipients of God's gracious love.

words but also a whole way of thinking about eternal truths. We hear some of these truths being said explicitly (e.g. "You shall not commit murder"), while others are said implicitly (e.g. the story of Joseph, in which we learn about God's sovereignty and human responsibility, even though these terms are not mentioned).

James Sire might say that we are trying to find out God's 'world view', but we could equally well describe it as discerning the mind of God, or seeking biblical principles behind the text of Scripture. Whatever we call it, the point is that when we read the Bible we are not only looking for what God says explicitly, but how God views reality. If we discover this, then we will know how to please him in situations different from the ones covered by the Bible passage.

If we follow the assumption that the original readership is Jewish, then it is fair to say that a surface reading of the book of Exodus, with its description of the rescue of Israel from Egypt, would lead a Jew to think that God's love is selective and particularly directed toward them. The next step is, of course, to think that it should be exclusively directed towards them.

Within the book of Jonah, there is only one Israelite who is mentioned and he is hardly the hero of the story. Jonah is the recipient of God's word and promises, and yet he is disobedient. He says he fears Yahweh but his fear seems pretty unconvincing beside the fear of the sailors. Jonah criticises those who forfeit the gracious love that could be theirs (2:8), and is a happy recipient of that love himself, but at the same time gets angry when people call on God's grace and God freely distributes it.

The situations they face

These matters lead me then to think that the structure and content of the book is deliberately arranged to have its Jewish readers asking themselves: "Am I like Jonah? Do I accept God's grace myself and yet want to cut others out from it? Is my view of God far too restricted?"

Feelings and actions

If this is the case, then it is easy to see what its impact might be. On the one hand, it would push some of its readers to repentance over their lack of God-like grace and mercy. For others, it would lead them to think that their deep hatred of foreigners is wrong. For others, it would lead them to actually reach out to those who have wronged them or who are their enemies, as God himself reaches out to his enemies. For others it might cause them to turn away from vain idols and remember God and the grace that could be theirs (2:8). For others it would cause them to stop running away from speaking God's word to the Gentiles and to do so knowing that such speaking may indeed be the way whereby God might demonstrate his grace and mercy, relenting from his fierce anger so that they might not perish.

Imagine for a moment that you are the original hearer/reader of your passage. Two things are happening to you as you listen/read. On the one hand, God comes to you in your situation and speaks to you. He challenges you to re-examine all that you are thinking and feeling in light of who he is and what his will is. On the other hand, you come with your own presuppositions about what God should or shouldn't be doing. You may be bent on listening and obeying or on closing your ears and rebelling.

In other words, as we draw together the threads of the passage, we should ask ourselves: How would this passage challenge or change the thoughts, actions, and feelings of the original readers? What might it have told them about:

- God?
- the world?
- themselves and other people?
- the situations that they face?

And what feelings and/or actions do you think it might have evoked in their particular situation?

hands on

1. Why is it important to do what we can to establish the purpose of a book of the Bible?

2. Write down the book or movie that has had the most impact upon you. Explain what that impact was. In what way did your thinking change as a result? Has it changed the way you act? What impact did it have on your emotions?

Step 5.1: Context

3. Why do you think the book of Titus was written?

4. What place does Titus 2:11-14 play in the thought of chapter 2 and the whole book?

hands on

Step 5.2: Summing up

5. What sort of impact do you think the book of Titus would have had on the original reader?

6. What do you think it would have taught Titus about:

God

the world

other people

the situations he was facing?

7. What sort of actions, feelings and responses do you think it was designed to evoke in him?

When we read the Bible there are two fundamental points that we need to hold together…

PTO

STEP

6

Determine other meanings

Step 6.1: Links

When we read the Bible there are two fundamental points that we need to hold together:

- that the Bible is the 'word of God' with a divine author;
- that the Bible is a human book, written by human beings in particular situations to other human beings in particular situations.

So far, we have spent most of our time looking at the 'human' side of the Bible (although I hope you've been remembering to pray for enlightenment as you've done so). We have attempted, where relevant, to get as much background information about the author and the original readers as we can in order to understand what God was saying to them. Now we need to turn more to the 'divine' nature of the Bible. You might remember that a number of implications sprang from our belief that the Bible was the 'word of God':

- The Bible was not only written for one group of people a long time ago. It was also written 'for us'.
- Because there is a divine author as well as a human author, it may sometimes be that there are other meanings intended by God but not intended by the original author.
- One piece of writing in the Bible does not stand on its own, it is part of a whole body of writing with the same divine author. There will be, therefore, various unifying strands running through it. The Bible 'hangs together'.
- True biblical interpretation must be done depending upon God for enlightenment. If we are to interpret the Bible accurately we must be in tune with the God who ultimately lies behind it. Our study of the Bible must be done in the context of prayer.
- The Bible will have implications for us today.
- We must stand under the Bible's authority. We must also have receptive hearts and wills that are determined to obey what we hear.

In Steps 6 and 7, we will deal with these implications in more depth.

How the Bible hangs together

When we look at how the Bible hangs together and at the links between one part of the Bible and another, we need to tread very carefully so that we handle the Scriptures rightly.

Concentric circles

First of all, we need to make sure that we work *in the right direction*. When we looked at the meaning of words (in Step 4), we saw that the best way to proceed was to work outwards in concentric circles. We placed the most weight on the most immediate context of a word, sentence or passage.

In looking for links between our passage and the rest of the Bible, we must work in the same manner. We must *start* with our passage. Then we can look at links between this passage and the rest of the book, then the author, then the Testament, then the Bible as a whole.

Links between parts of the Bible

We also need to know what sort of links we are looking for and how to find them. One Bible scholar[1] has helpfully outlined how we should forge links between the Old and New Testaments. His suggestions are also useful in working out links between any passage of Scripture and the rest of the Bible. He suggests that the following links need to be kept in mind:

1. *The continuous history of God's people and the picture of God's dealings with mankind.* For example, Exodus 15 tells us how the Israelites sang the Song of Moses in response to God's rescue from the Egyptians. This passage is linked to God's repeated rescues in the past (e.g. Noah) and in the future (e.g. the crossing of the Jordan by Joshua, the rescue from exile in Babylon, and the rescue from the seven last plagues in Revelation 15).

2. *The way one Scripture is quoted in another part of the Bible.* For example, the phrase "out of Egypt did I call my son" in Hosea

---

1 Gerhard Hasel in his book *Old Testament Theology: Basic Issues in the Current Debate* (Eerdmans, Grand Rapids, 1972), pp. 125ff.

11:1 has direct links with the New Testament–it's quoted in Matthew 2:15. It also has strong links with history and the way God deals with his people (see point 1).

3. *The use of common theological key terms (e.g. creation, judgement, grace)*. For example, in Hebrews 2-6, key terms such as 'rest', 'Sabbath', 'faith', 'judgement' and 'expiation' are mentioned. All rely heavily for their meaning on the Old Testament use of these terms.

4. *The use of major themes (e.g. the kingship of God, people of God, exodus experience, election, covenant, judgement, salvation, bondage, redemption)*. Even if the actual words are not used, one passage in the Bible may be linked with others through a vast network of major themes. For example, 'the kingdom of God' is mentioned time and time again in the ministry of Jesus. A concordance would reveal that the actual *term* occurs relatively infrequently both before and after the ministry of Jesus. However, the *theme* is evident from the first three chapters of the Bible through to the last three.

5. *The fact of promise/prediction and its fulfilment*. One of the things which distinguishes our God from pagan gods is that "he declares the things to come beforehand" (Isa 41:22). He is a God who utters promises and whom we can trust to fulfil them. Thus, throughout the Bible, we see a constant thread of 'promise' or 'prediction' and its fulfilment. For example, when Daniel reflects on the 'seventy years' in Daniel 9, we should look both backwards to passages that promise judgement on Israel and a 70-year exile, and forwards to the New Testament where the fulfilment of these promises is seen in the ministry of Jesus.

6. *The progress of God's saving history*. As Christians, we believe that God has revealed himself in history through particular events and the theological interpretation of these events. This revelation of God is progressive. If we were to start at the beginning of the Bible and read to the end, we would see this 'salvation history' traced out in a series of significant

events (creation; fall; God's promise to Abraham; the exodus from Egypt; the covenant given through Moses; the entry into the Promised Land; the Davidic monarchy; the exile; the restoration; the birth, death, resurrection and ascension of Christ; the consummation of the world). The pinnacle of this salvation history is the person and work of Christ.

We should ask ourselves how each passage fits into God's overall plan for his world and into the supreme revelation of himself in Christ. For example, the story of Abraham in Genesis 12:1-3 can be seen as part of the continued cycle of sin and salvation in Genesis 1-11, and as a pattern and plan for the final salvation in Christ. The appendix suggests some good books to help you with this approach to the Bible.

Getting down to work

How do we put these ideas into practice? We need to go through each of the six areas just outlined and sort out if there are any grounds for making links with other parts of the Bible. In other words, we need to ask ourselves:

1. How and where does this passage fit into the overall history of God's people?

   This is done by looking at other parts of the Bible that address this particular period or incident and by asking: "Where else in the Bible do similar events happen? Are there any links between this incident and others?"

2. Is this passage quoted directly elsewhere in the Bible?

   If it is quoted elsewhere we need to ask: "Why is it quoted? How does the author understand it? Is the interpretation of it any different to the meaning it seems to have in its original context?". A good cross-reference Bible should quickly and easily put you onto direct quotations as well as allusions in other parts of the Bible.

3. Given the work I have already done on key theological terms (in Step 4: Word meanings), what weight should I put on their use in this passage and other passages in the Bible?

You have already done some work on what particular passages mean and how they are used in the rest of the Bible. Ask yourself if these words are significant in the passage. Do the links they have with other parts of the Bible shed light on the overall meaning?

4. Are any major biblical themes touched on in this passage?

We should also be asking: "Are there any key biblical themes which are implied? What theological background is presumed in the passage? Is there any development of the theme here? How does the theme develop throughout the

---

example

In the following example we have applied the six questions to the book of Jonah.

1. History

The historical references to the book have already been stated. They refer to a time when the Assyrian nation was one of the dominant world powers but was also at a particularly low ebb.

It is probably worth pointing out that Jonah is a prophet from the northern tribes, that is, from the part of Israel which was decimated by the Assyrian nation in 722 BC and dispersed throughout the Assyrian kingdom.

2. Quotation

Just as Jonah appears to be dependent on a tradition that goes back at least as far as Exodus 34:6 (cf. Ps 86:5; Joel 2:13), so the book of Jonah itself is quoted in other parts of the Bible (Matt 12:38-41; 16:1-4; Lk 11:29-32). The New Testament references are mainly concerned with the teaching of Jesus and his references to the sign of Jonah.

Although the references to the sign of Jonah are difficult, the main idea appears to relate to Jonah's miraculous deliverance from death in the fish. It is as

though Jesus is saying something like, "Like Jonah, I will appear alive again after three days. I will be rescued by God, I will preach a message of repentance and whoever responds to that message will be saved (whether Jew or Gentile".

3. Key terms

As I've indicated previously, the key terms appear to be gathered around the words 'grace' and 'love', which we've already done some work on, although the more I think about it, the more I think it is going to be necessary to do some further work before we wrap up the impact of this book.

4. Major themes

There are a number of major themes within the book. First, there is the theme of the word of God and its impact on all of life (seen in its impact on Jonah, on the fish, on Nineveh, etc.). Second, there is the theme of the sovereignty of God (seen in his rule over the fish of the sea, over the sea and the dry land, over the nations, over the future of Israel, etc.). Third, there is the theme of the Gentiles in comparison with the Jews (the Gentiles seem to be treated very positively by the author. He shows them

Bible, and how does this passage fit into that development?"

5. Are there any promises given or fulfilled in this passage?

   If there are promises given, we need to ascertain when they are fulfilled, how, and whether the fulfilment completely lives up to expectations. Further, we should look for multiple fulfilments. If the passage refers back to a promise, we need to ascertain when the promise was given, and whether this passage is a fulfilment or merely a reminder or adaptation of the promise.

---

responding to God, while Jonah seems to be portrayed negatively). Fourth, there is the love of God for all his creatures whether they be cattle, Gentiles or Jews.

5. Promise/fulfilment

The main promise touched on in this passage is God's nature to be "slow to anger, abounding in steadfast love, and one who relents from punishing". This promise can be relied on, not only by Jews (to whom it was originally given) but also by Gentiles.

6. Salvation history

The book of Jonah does appear to represent a new revelation of God, or at least a clarification of how a previous revelation had been interpreted. When we read the early part of the Bible we read about God's choice of Abraham and his descendants, the Israelites. Because of God's special act of grace in choosing them, they became his special people, his treasured possession out of all the peoples (Exod 19:5).

The problem with being special to God is that you begin to think he doesn't have any other interests. You tie God into your own world and resent his actions

elsewhere. This appears to happen to Israel at times. They concentrate more on God as the one who saves *Israel* than on him being the Creator of *all the earth*.

Jonah addresses this type of thinking and challenges it. The book tells us of a God whose compassion is for all and therefore whose deliverance is for all. Moreover, it rebukes those who think that it is okay to be vindictive toward the other people of the world.

Therefore, the book raises issues already present in God's revelation of himself and pushes them to the surface. He is the God of all the earth. His purpose is to save Gentiles as well as Jews. His nature pushes him this way. At this point we have begun to move into the world of the New Testament and to many of the themes raised there time and time again (e.g. the gospel breaking down the dividing wall between Jew and Gentile, etc.).

As we have answered each of the questions in this section, it has been hard not to follow the ideas through. We are now beginning to answer the question: How does this passage fit into the whole Bible?

6. How does this passage fit into God's overall plan of salvation?

This is a fundamental question in biblical interpretation. It involves working out whether or not this passage represents a new step or a regression in God's plan. We should especially ask how our knowledge of God's purpose in Jesus helps us understand this passage and its implications. Why do you think this passage is here? What was God's purpose in having it written?

Having got all this information, we now need to put it together. This is the purpose of our next step.

Step 6.2: Biblical context

When we come to the Bible, we come as Christians. As Christians, we have come to believe in Jesus Christ and acknowledge that he is the Lord of all. We have pledged our allegiance to him and given our whole beings over to the worship of him. We have also come to see that he is the centre of all God's purposes–the word of God *par excellence.*

Because we are believers in Jesus and in God's purpose revealed in him, we have certain convictions about the Bible. We are convinced that:

- the Bible is to be treated as a unity
- the Bible has a purpose
- the centre of God's purpose as revealed in the Bible is found in the person and work of Jesus.

Each of these convictions has implications for how we treat the Bible.

The unity of the Bible

Christians understand that the Old Testament is incomplete. It waits for an end, it holds out a hope for the future. On the other hand, Christians also understand that the New Testament is built on the Old Testament and is unintelligible without it. Louis

Berkhof, in his book *Principles of Biblical Interpretation*, has summarised some of the implications this has for us as we read the Bible. He says that in the interpretation of the Old and New Testaments, we should be guided by the following considerations:

- the Old Testament offers the key to the right interpretation of the New.
- the New Testament is a commentary on the Old.
- on the one hand, the interpreter should be aware of minimising the Old Testament.
- on the other hand, he should guard against reading too much into the Old Testament.

We could represent this diagrammatically as follows:

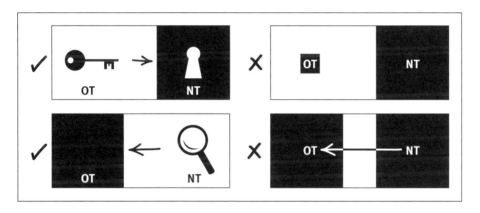

The Purpose of the Bible

Christians not only approach the Bible as a united whole, they also consider it to be a book with a purpose. This was how Paul urged Timothy to read the Bible and it is how we should all read it.

> *But as for you, continue in what you have learned and have become convinced of, because you know those from whom you learned it, and how from infancy you have known the holy Scriptures, which are able to make you wise for salvation through faith in Christ Jesus.*
>
> *2 Timothy 3:14-15*

As we read the Bible, we are to keep in mind the purpose for which it was written. It was written "to make us wise for salvation"– its purpose is salvation. In other words, the Bible aims to deliver humanity from evil and into fellowship with God. This purpose is carried out as the Bible tells us how God has been active in his world and what his acts mean.

Earlier in our method, we observed that every interpreter of the Bible needs to have a general grasp of history and geography to fully understand the Bible. However, each Bible student should also aim to have an overall feel for the Bible in terms of its theology: what it reveals about God and his purpose and how that purpose unfolds. We need to ask: How does God reveal himself progressively to his people? What is the process of God's self revelation and plan of salvation as recorded in the Bible?

example

As I have worked on Jonah more and more, I have become convinced that the quotation of Exodus 34 in Jonah 4:2 holds the key for interpreting the book. I decided to go back and take a good look at the passage in Exodus.

Then the LORD came down in the cloud and stood there with him and proclaimed his name, the LORD. And he passed in front of Moses, proclaiming, "The LORD, the LORD, the compassionate and gracious God, slow to anger, abounding in love and faithfulness, maintaining love to thousands, and forgiving wickedness, rebellion and sin. Yet he does not leave the guilty unpunished; he punishes the children and their children for the sin of the fathers to the third and fourth generation."

Exodus 34:5-7

He prayed to the Lord, "O Lord, is this not what I said when I was still at home? That is why I was so quick to flee to Tarshish. I knew that you are a gracious and compassionate God, slow to anger and abounding in love, a God who relents from sending calamity."

Jonah 4:2

When I typed out the two passages and put them side by side I couldn't help but notice the difference. The stress on God's forgiveness that is obvious in the Exodus passage in that he maintains love to thousands (of generations?) is pushed even harder in the Jonah passage. This fits in with our conclusions about the meaning and purpose of the book from a number of different perspectives.

At this point I decided that I'd better do some more work on the other references to 'grace' or 'gracious' in the NIV. By looking up some commentaries I found that the word used in 2:8 is actually the same word used in 4:2.

All of a sudden, the book began to fall into place for me. The book was a book about God's 'lovingkindness'. As a Jew, Jonah knew that God is a God of lovingkindness. He knew this from Exodus

It is not difficult to construct a broad outline. God reveals himself firstly in his creation. His revelation reaches its climax in Jesus Christ and its conclusion in the consummation of the world when he sets up a new heaven and a new earth. However, gradually we need to fill in the gaps between these three points and make clear what such things tell us about God. This will give us a feel for how the whole Bible hangs together .

More than this, if we accept that the purpose of the Bible is to bring people to salvation, this will shape our interpretation. We will understand that separate books of the Bible are organically related to each other. They are united in what they think God is doing in his world and how he does it. We will ask ourselves how particular passages teach us about God's purpose of salvation and how they fit into that overall purpose.

34:6. But he also knew Exodus 34:7, that is, that God punishes the wicked. From the experience of the history of Israel, and even from his own experience, he knew that God's mercy and love triumph over his judgement (i.e. he is a God whose love extends to thousands of generations). However, what he feared was that if this really was the character of God, then it couldn't be restricted to Israel or to those within the covenant. This, he says, is why he fled to Tarshish in the very beginning. Deep down he knew that the Lord was a God of love who relents from sending calamity.

The book of Jonah is saying in crystal clear terms that Jonah's fears were justified. God saves the sailors and the Ninevites as well as Jonah. The point is made in Jonah 2:8 in the NIV. God's grace can even be the experience of those who cling to worthless idols if they wish to call upon it. For at the core of his nature, God's desire is to save. Salvation comes from him (2:9).

At this point I reflected on the impact of the New Testament and the person of Jesus.

• *The New Testament tells me that God's greatest act of grace and love has happened and been clearly seen. He has sent his own Son into the world to be born, live and die as a human being. He has been crucified that the world might be forgiven. Moreover, that love has reached outside the community of Israel to Samaritans, black Ethiopian eunuchs (Acts 8), Gentiles (Acts 10-11), and even to me.*

• *The New Testament also makes clear that those who have seen God's grace and love in Jesus should not be like Jonah, who is happy to receive God's love and grace but not so happy to reflect it in his own attitudes and actions. I must do more than pagans and tax collectors in the way I live. I must be perfect as my heavenly Father is perfect (Matt 5:38-48). I should forgive even as I've been forgiven (Matt 18:21-35; Eph 4:25-5:2) and accept others even as I have been accepted (Rom 15:7-13).*

The centre of the Bible

We believe that the centre of both Testaments, and the link between them, is the person and work of Jesus. This was Jesus' own understanding and that of his followers (e.g. Jn 5:39-40; Lk 24:44-47; Heb 1:1-4). When the authors of the New Testament look at the Old Testament, they see Jesus as the 'key' to understanding it (e.g. Mk 12:1-11; Gal 3:16).

The implication for us is plain: when we read the Scriptures, we must let them point us in the right direction. We must see that they teach us about God's purpose of salvation as revealed in the person and work of Jesus. They bear witness to him. We must receive that witness and come to him that we might have life.

However, it would be wrong to think that Jesus and the New Testament writers didn't allow the Old Testament to speak for itself. For example, Jesus urges the Pharisees to act mercifully on the grounds of the plain meaning of Micah 6:6-8 (see Matt 9:13), and the New Testament authors told the children of Gentile parents that they should obey their parents just as the Old Testament urged them to (Eph 6:1-3).

---

example

As I thought further about the New Testament, I was struck by the so-called *Parable of the Lost Son* in Luke 15. According to Luke 15:1-2, this parable and the ones immediately before it (The Parable of the Lost Sheep and The Parable of the Lost Coin) were told in response to the Pharisees and teachers of the law who were critical of Jesus welcoming sinners and eating with them. The Parable of the Lost Son tells how the father is overflowing in his love for the son who has strayed. His love goes beyond commonly accepted norms of behaviour and far beyond any expectations the son might have had of him. It is spontaneous and generous. On the other side, the older son is strikingly similar to Jonah and the Pharisees. He is a beneficiary of the father's generosity but resentful when that generosity is exercised freely.

As you can see, at this point I have begun to put the book into a much larger context and am well on the way to seeing what impact the book of Jonah has for me in my own situation, helped on by other parts of the Bible that address similar issues.

Because we are Christians, we must interpret the Bible in the light of these two facts:

- the Bible as a whole must be seen for what it is a witness to Jesus
- the Old Testament must be allowed to speak for itself; it must not be always read through the New Testament.

Putting it all together

When all this is put together we should ask ourselves the following sorts of questions as we look at a passage of Scripture:

- What place does this passage play in the whole Bible?
- How does it fit into God's plan of salvation as displayed in Jesus?
- What does it add to what we already know about God and his purpose?
- How would the message of the Bible be less complete if this passage did not exist?
- How does this passage 'bear witness to Jesus'?
- How does it function as part of the whole Bible?
- How about other Christians?

When we study the Bible we are not the only people doing so. Other Christians in all ages have studied the passages that we have studied and have studied them in lesser or greater detail than we have.

These people, who have the same presuppositions as us and the same Spirit, can be of great assistance. We ought not to be embarrassed to compare our conclusions with theirs, and to see if they have reached different conclusions. We can do this by consulting their commentaries and other writings.

hands on

1. Look again at the list of ways to link a passage with other parts of the Bible. Do you understand how to put each one into practice? Discuss as a group any difficulties you might have.

2. Think about the last sermon you heard on the Old Testament. How did it link the Old Testament with the New Testament (if it did)? Did it fit in with any of the ways suggested in this session?

3. Look back over my examples from the book of Jonah. Does my analysis of the purpose of the book ring true? Does it fit the facts?

Step 6.1: Links

4. Take out your now much-marked copy of the book of Titus and your notes on it. Read Titus 2 and think through the six possible types of links you might find in this chapter. (Note that some of the questions may not be suitable for this passage. In that case don't force it.)

1. History

2. Quotation

3. Key terms

4. Major themes

5. Promise/fulfilment

6. Salvation history

hands on

Step 6.2: Biblical context

Take another look at chapter 2 in Titus. What place does it have in the thought of the whole Bible?

Check out some commentaries or dictionaries that mention Titus. See what they think of the book and how their analysis of the message of chapter 2 compares with yours.

This is what good Bible reading is all about: discovering how God would have us act in our situation.

PTO

STEP

7

Determine the impact

The problem of application

*"But we are not going to have our wives dress like prosti-
tutes," protested an elder in the Ngbaka church in northern
Congo, as he replied to the suggestion made by the missionary
that the women should be required to wear blouses to cover
their breasts. The church leaders were unanimous in objecting
to such a requirement, for in that part of Congo the well-
dressed and fully-dressed African women were too often
prostitutes, since they alone had the money to spend on attrac-
tive garments. Different peoples are in wide disagreement as
to the amount or type of clothes required for modesty. Not long
ago one of the chiefs in the Micronesian island of Yap forbade
any woman coming into the town with a blouse. However, he
insisted that all women would have to wear grass skirts
reaching almost to their ankles. To the Yapese way of thinking, bare legs are a sign of immodesty, while the uncovered
breasts are perfectly proper.* [1]

Eugene Nida

What would you do in this situation? What would God do?
Which is the right way: to endorse the principle of modesty and
accept bare breasts but covered legs? Or to insist that the Western
understanding of modesty is correct?

The way ahead is to press for the timeless biblical principle of
modesty, even though it might express itself very differently in
different situations. This is what good Bible reading is all about:
discovering how God would have us act in our situation.

And that's very difficult, isn't it? After all, we cannot avoid the
fact that there is a gap between us and the writers of the Bible.
The gap is not only one of time. We are separated at least in some
ways by culture, language, world view and customs. The writers
of Scripture don't give us a message free of cultural baggage.
We must travel back into their times, as best we can, and do the

---

1   From Eugene Nida's book *Customs and Cultures: Anthropology of Christian Missions,*
     (Harper and Row, New York, 1954), p.1.

cultural baggage stripping ourselves. It's a sort of reverse missionary voyage.

This is what we have been doing so far in *Postcard from Palestine.* Although we haven't stopped being people of our own background, time and culture, we have tried to make sure that we are adequately briefed on the background and circumstances of the original hearers and readers. We have crossed cultures while still in our lounge rooms and said to ourselves: "What was it like for them? How would they have received this message? How would it have changed the way they thought, acted and felt?"

But at the same time, we need to recognise that we are not people of the 6th century BC or the 1st century AD. We are people of our own time and culture who can never be completely divorced from our own situation. Nevertheless, by making sure we are adequately briefed on the situation of the original hearers and readers we minimise the risk of taking the message of the Bible out of context and misapplying it to our own situation. Having done this exercise, it is now time to take what we have learnt–the ideas, principles, attitudes and feelings–and see what they mean in our own situation. It is time to ask ourselves: "Given my situation, how can I be most faithful to the message I have heard, in my time and place? How should I change the way I think, act and feel? What does God want me to do here and now?"

In other words, we have finally come to 'apply' what we have learnt.

The process of application flows on from what we have already done in our earlier Steps. Our understanding of the nature of the Bible and the way God reveals himself to us in the Scriptures will determine how we apply it to our own situation. In this final step we ask ourselves:

- What does this passage tell us about:
  God?
  the world?
  ourselves and other people?
  the situations that we face?
- Are there areas where I need to change my thinking as a result of what I've learnt?

- What feelings and/or actions should it evoke in my/our particular situation?

Notice how these questions are almost identical to those we asked earlier (in Step 6.2: Summing up). But there have been some changes since we put ourselves in the place of the original hearers. It will be helpful for us to analyse what has changed and what is still the same.

Some things change

Firstly, we have the benefit of looking at what the whole Bible has to say on things mentioned in the passage. In other words, we

examples

Last time we looked at the book of Jonah, I noted that I thought that the book was an exposition of God's lovingkindness. We noted that at the very core of God's nature is his mercy or grace and how Jonah knew this for himself and his people but was not sure that he could live with its implications for the wider world.

The things I learn about God, the world, myself and other people have therefore been much the same as what Jonah learnt. From reading Jonah I've learnt the same things as the original readers learnt.

I've learnt that God is the creator of all the world, that he is a God who is gracious and spontaneous in his love for me and also for the rest of the world. His love is not selective and therefore I should not be surprised if it is directed to those outside the people of God.

But what of the impact of the passage for me? What of those other two questions:

• Are there areas where I need to change my thinking as a result of what I've learnt?
• What feelings and/or actions should it evoke in my/our particular situation?

Now is the time to get personal. As I examine myself and my situation I realise that I'm not as far away from Jonah or the Pharisees of Luke 15 as I should be. I know the orthodox statements about God. I can say along with Jonah that "I fear the Lord, the God of heaven, who made the sea and the dry land" and I know, along with Jonah, that God is "a gracious God and merciful, slow to anger, and abounding in steadfast love, and ready to relent from punishing". Moreover, like Jonah I have experienced God's mercy myself.

But my problem is that I am constantly in danger of failing to act like God in my dealings with others. God's tendency is always for his mercy to triumph over his judgement whereas mine, like Jonah's, is for judgement to triumph over mercy. I am less forgiving than God, less long-suffering than God, less gracious than God.

This passage calls on me to repent and change. It drives me back to the cross to re-examine my status before God and his great forgiveness of me. It then drives me to my neighbour to love him and her even as God has loved me. Practically this means that the person who has wronged me needs to be have some added information. This is most marked where the original hearers were before Christ and the New Testament. What they knew in shadow we now know in reality (Col 2.17).

The second thing that has changed is our world and the situations that we face every day. We live in a very different world: they spoke in Hebrew, Aramaic or Greek, while we speak in English; they fought with spears, swords, bows and arrows while we do so with nuclear weapons; they thought the world was flat while we think it to be almost spherical; they faced Roman oppressors while most of us face nothing worse than the tax man, the oppressive boss, or the examiner.

---

forgiven. If I can't do that without speaking to them, then I need to make sure I do.

This is an application of Jonah to me, personally. However, having arrived at this point it is probably helpful that I move on to the next step which is strictly speaking not the purpose of this book—the question of how I implement change as a result of interpreting and applying Scripture.

Experience has taught me that unless I turn my thoughts into action they remain just thoughts. Experience has also taught me that one great aid in obedience is making myself accountable to another Christian. For these reasons, what I need to do at this stage is to talk with a friend about what I've found in the book of Jonah, write down and show them how I resolve to change as a result, and ask them to pray for me as I put these things into practice and to enquire occasionally about how I'm going.

Of course there are other applications of this passage apart from the one I have talked about. For example, the book of Jonah could rightly be applied as an encouragement toward forgiveness within the Christian community, or as an encouragement toward evangelism among those who don't know Christ. As a preacher it might be appropriate for me to stress other applications with different audiences, but what I was doing here was talking about what was important for me as an interpreter of the Bible in my own study. What was important was how the Scripture, rightly interpreted, was used by God to strike me in its freshness where I currently am.

Some stay the same

For a start, God hasn't changed. He is still the same today, yesterday and forever. The things a passage teaches us about God will be similar to the things it taught the original hearers. Our picture may be fuller due to additional information, but the things we learn about our God are still the same, whether we live in the 8th century BC or the 20th century AD.

Secondly, our culture, customs, language, technology and world view may be different, but there are some crucial similarities between us and the original hearers. We are still the creation of God. We are still inheritors of and willing participants in Adam's fall; sinful human beings in constant rebellion against our creator. We still "suppress the truth of God in unrighteousness" and seek every way we can to justify ourselves before God.

Further, our world is much like the world in which the original hearers lived. It is still corrupted by our sin and in a mess as a result. It is still "groaning in travail", longing to be set free from its slavery to futility (see Rom 8:18f). We still do not see humans acting as they should and exercising the rule of God as they should.

The similarities are profound, and we need to be wary of magnifying the differences between us and the original hearers. *On most occasions, the similarities between us and the original hearers are central and the differences peripheral. The original hearers of the Bible are very like us and we are very like them.*

Hence, when we put these similarities and differences together we should realise that what God says today through the passage will be very much the same as it was for the original hearers. The answers we find here in Step 7 will be the same as in Step 6.2. Because the answers are identical, it is inevitable that our actions and obedience will also be expressed very similarly. For example, as God tells us that he is the creator of the world who stands in judgement over his sinful creation, we, like the original hearers, should repent and call upon the name of Christ for salvation. Or again, as God tells us that we should submit to governing authorities, we will respect and honour our rulers, pay our taxes and obey where obedience is due, just as the original hearers did.

On the other hand, we need to realise that our situation is somewhat different to that of the original hearers and that the change in thinking that occurs in us may be different, just as our actions and feelings may be expressed differently. For example, as God tells us to be modest, we should rightly express that in a way that is meaningful in our own situation.

hands on

1. One of our great problems in reading the Bible is working out when a particular statement reflects something in the culture and therefore should apply differently to us.

Discuss the application of the following passages, in light of what we have learnt in this chapter:

• Titus 2:9-10

• 1 Corinthians 11:1-10

• Hebrews 13:1-8

hands on

Step 7: Determine the impact

2. Take a final look at Titus 2. What is its significance for you in your situation? Work through the questions in this step.

• What does this passage tell us about:

God

the world

ourselves and other people

the situations we face

• Are there areas where I need to change my thinking as a result of what I've learnt?

• What feelings and/or actions should it evoke in my/our particular situation?

3. Prepare a short talk for your Bible study group that explains Titus 2 and applies it to their situation.

Appendices

.۱

further reading

The following key applies to all the following lists and categories of books:

- A good basic book to start with
- ■ A more in-depth book, should you want to pursue things further
- ▲ A fairly technical book

General books on interpreting the Bible

- Arnold, Jeffrey. *Discovering the Bible for Yourself. (A Lifeguide Handbook)*, Downers Grove: InterVarsity Press, 1993
- Blanchard, John. *How to Enjoy Your Bible*, Hertfordshire: Evangelical Press, 1984
- ■ Fee, Gordon D & Douglas Stuart. *How to Read the Bible for all its Worth*, Grand Rapids: Scripture Union, 1982
- ▲ Fee, Gordon D. *New Testament Exegesis: A Handbook for Students and Pastors*, (Revised Edition), Louisville: Westminster/John Knox, 1993
- Stott, John R. W. *Understanding the Bible*, Homebush West: Anzea, 1972
- ▲ Stuart, Douglas. *Old Testament Exegesis: A Primer for Students and Pastors*, Philadephia: Westminster, 1980
- Wright, Chris. *User's Guide to the Bible*, Herts: Lion, 1984

The authority and inspiration of Scripture

- Packer, J. I. *Freedom, Authority, and Scripture*, Leicester: Inter-Varsity Press, 1981
- ■ Packer, J. I. *God has Spoken*, (Updated and expanded edition), London: Hodder and Stoughton, 1993
- ■ Wenham, John. *Christ and the Bible*, Guildford: Eagle, 1993

Modern literary theory (general)

- ● Gallagher, Susan V. and Roger Lundin. *Literature Through the Eyes of Faith*, New York: Harper Collins, 1989
- ▲ Lodge, David (ed). *20th Century Literary Criticism: A Reader*, Harlow: Longman, 1972
- ▲ Lodge, David (ed). *Modern Criticism and Theory: A Reader*, Harlow: Longman, 1988

Modern literary theory and the Bible

- ■ Longman III, Tremper. *Literary Approaches to Biblical Interpretation* (Foundations of Contemporary Interpretation, Volume 3), Grand Rapids: Academie, 1987
- ▲ Lundin, Roger, Anthony Thistleton and Clarence Walhout. *The Responsibility of Hermeneutics*, Grand Rapids: Eerdmans, 1985
- ■ Tate, W. Randolph. *Biblical Interpretation: An Integrated Approach*, Peabody: Hendrickson, 1991
- ▲ Thistleton, Anthony C. *The Two Horizons: New Testament Hermeneutics and Philosophical Description with Special Reference to Heidegger, Bultmann, Gadamer, and Wittgenstein*, Exeter: Paternoster, 1980
- ▲ Thistleton, Anthony C. *New Horizons in Hermeneutics: The Theory and Practice of Transforming Biblical Reading*, London: Harper Collins, 1992

Genre analysis and interpretation

- ● Ryken, Leland. *How to Read the Bible as Literature...and Get More Out of It*, Grand Rapids: Academie, 1984
- ■ Green, Joel B. *How to Read Prophecy*, Leicester: Inter-Varsity Press, 1984
- ■ Green, Joel B. *How to Read the Gospels and Acts*, Downers Grove: InterVarsity Press, 1987
- ▲ Blomberg, Craig L. *Interpreting the Parables*, Leicester: Apollos, 1990

Background information

▲ Bright, John. *A History of Israel,* (Second Edition), Towbridge and Esher: Westminster, 1972

● Bruce, F. F. *Israel and the Nations,* Exeter: Paternoster, 1963

● Jenkins, Simon. *Bible Mapbook,* Herts: Lion, 1985

■ Thompson, J. A. *Handbook of Life in Bible Times,* Leicester: Inter-Varsity Press, 1986

Biblical theology

▲ Dumbrell, William J. *The Faith of Israel: Its Expression in the Books of the Old Testament,* Leicester: Apollos, 1988

● Goldsworthy, Graeme. *Gospel and Kingdom,* Exeter: Paternoster, 1981

■ Goldsworthy, Graeme. *According to Plan: The Unfolding Revelation of God in the Bible,* Leicester: Inter-Varsity Press, 1991

■ Strom, Mark. *Days Are Coming: Exploring Biblical Patterns,* Rydalmere: Hodder and Stoughton, 1989

Application

● Kuhatschek, Jack. *Taking the Guesswork out of Applying the Bible,* Leicester: Inter-Varsity Press, 1990

▲ Larkin, William J. Jnr. *Culture and Biblical Hermeneutics: Interpreting and Applying the Authoritative Word in a Relativistic Age,* Grand Rapids: Baker, 1988

an overview of biblical geography

There are three important geographical areas in the Bible. The first, the Fertile Crescent, is important because it is from here that Abraham first came. It is also the source of repeated threats to Israel. The second, Egypt, is important because it is the place in which the most formative event in Israel's history took place–the Exodus. The third is Palestine itself, the centre stage of the story of the Bible.

A book well worth purchasing as an aid to understanding the geography of the Bible as it is linked with the principal people, places and events is Simon Jenkin's *Bible Mapbook* (Lion, 1985).

The Fertile Crescent (Map 1)

A line drawn from Ur through Haran and then down the Syrian coast as far as Egypt traces out a crescent. The narrow strip around this line is called the Fertile Crescent. This strip is rich in water and is therefore the centre of farming and the path which trade routes follow. For the same reasons, it is also the route along which armies travel to wage war.

Egypt

The Jews find their identity as God's people in a series of events closely connected with the land of Egypt and the area between Egypt and Palestine. It was here that the Exodus took place, and it was also to here that the last remnants of the southern kingdom retreated in 587 BC.

Palestine (Maps 2 & 3)

The centre of activity as far as Israel and biblical history is concerned is the piece of land which we know as Palestine. Compared with Australia, Palestine is tiny. It is a narrow piece of land some 300-400 km long (if we include the desert regions in the south), and anything from 50-80 km wide.

The area has been traditionally divided into four geographical subdivisions running from North to South. Each of these strips of land becomes higher the further North you travel and drier and less able to be cultivated the further South you travel. From West to East these strips are knows as: the Coastal Plain, the Western Hills, the Rift Valley and the Eastern Hills.

The Coastal Plain

The Coastal Plain extends for some 200 km from Gaza and the desert (Negev) in the South, to the borders of Lebanon. It is interrupted by Mount Carmel (the battlefield of Elijah and the prophets of Baal in 1 Kings 18). The plain of Asher to the North played no major role in Israelite history. The same cannot be said for the plain of Jezreel, a tract of land 50 km long and 20 km wide. This valley formed the main route from Egypt to Damascus in the North and so was the site of many strategic battles (e.g. Judg 4-5; 11; 1 Sam 29; 32; 2 Kgs 23). It is also the scene of the last great battle of history, the battle of Armageddon (literally, "the mountain of Megiddo"– Rev 16:16).

To the south of Carmel lies the plain of Dor and the plain of Sharon. The latter was the home of the Philistines (from which the name 'Palestine' is drawn) with their five major cities of Ekron, Asdod, Ashkelon, Gath and Gaza. Further south the plain is separated from the mountains by the hill lands of the Shephelah. This 'hill country' which formed a buffer between Israel and Philistia forms the setting for much of the book of Joshua, various Judges and the life of David.

The Western Hills

The Western Hills are the central highlands of Palestine. They stretch some 300 km from northern Galilee to the Sinai. In Lebanon to the North, famous for its cedars, this range rises to over 1800 m above sea level. The highest peak in Palestine is in the North, Jebal Jermap (1208 m). Lower Galilee consists of a number of east-to-west ridges, none of which rises above 600 m.

This area, hardly mentioned in the Old Testament, becomes the centre of attention in much of the New Testament, especially the Gospels. These mountains are broken by the plains of Jezreel and Megiddo which form an easy passage from north to south.

The centre of this strip takes in the important towns of Shechem, Shiloh, Bethel and Samaria. Together with other fertile basins, Samaria was exposed to outside influences and was therefore easily enticed away from faithful allegiance to God.

Further south, Samaria merges into Judea, studded by the familiar cities of Jerusalem, Bethlehem and Hebron. In light of the history of Israel, it is interesting to note that Samaria was fairly accessible, whereas Judea was more isolated from outside contact. The slopes are steeper and more difficult to traverse, and there is little reason to cross them since the passage east is blocked by the Dead Sea.

The Rift Valley

The Rift Valley cuts a deep hole right through the centre of Palestine, starting at the foothills of Mt Hermon. This mountain, whose snow-capped peaks provide the source of the Jordan (Deut 3:9; 4:48), is not far from the town of Dan which was considered the uppermost extent of Israelite territory. The Jordan, which flows all year, cuts through the Lake of Tiberias (or Sea of Galilee) some 200 metres below sea level. This lake, with its cities of Chorazin, Capernaum and Bethsaida was the main site for much of Jesus' early ministry.

From here the river, fed by intermittent rivers, winds through a narrow flood plain covered with thick scrub (the jungle of Jeremiah 17:5) to the Dead Sea (391 metres below sea level). This sea is known as Dead because the only water which leaves there leaves by evaporation, thus leaving an accumulation of minerals behind. The Rift Valley continues south through the desert of the Arabah.

The Eastern Hills

The Eastern Hills, also known as the Transjordan, are cut by four important rivers: the Yarmuk, Jabbok, Arnon and Zered. They receive considerable rain and are fertile. However, the further east one travels the less rain there is, and before long the fertile land turns to desert. The fertile strip reaches its widest point in Bashan, known today as the Golan Heights. Across this part runs a road from Damascus to Lake Galilee, providing an important route into or out of Palestine. Further south we find Gilead and then the plateau which was the home of the Ammonites and Moabites.

Map 1

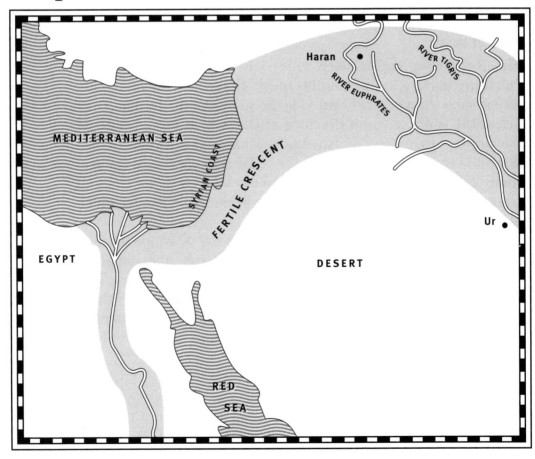

Map 2: Palestine *(showing major Old and New Testament locations)*

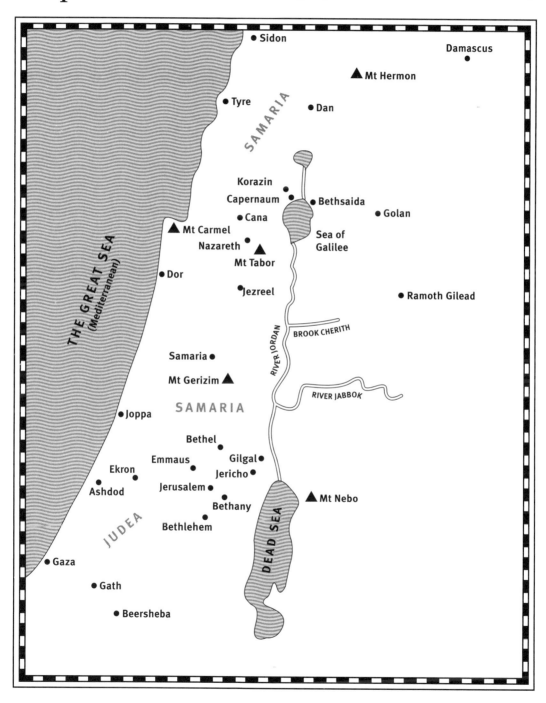

Map 3: Topographical cross-section of Palestine

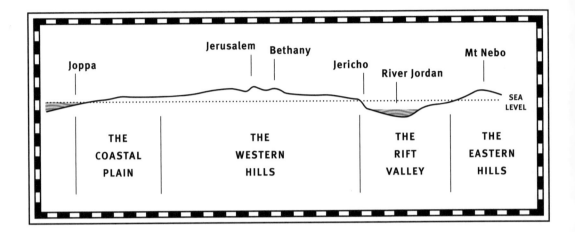

an introduction to interpretation

In a book designed to get everyone reading the Bible 'hands-on', we have had to leave to one side some of the more complicated issues involved in biblical interpretation. In this short appendix, I suggest a useful approach to these more theoretical issues.

Finding the right focus for our attention

I love the paintings of the Impressionists and so it was with great anticipation that I waited in the queue some time ago to see an exhibition of their work that was travelling through Australia. I remember standing in front of one particular painting–'Luncheon of the Boating Party' by Auguste Renoir–and being unable to move away from it. Until that moment all I had seen was coloured or even black and white photos, not much larger than postcards. I was not prepared for a painting two metres wide and one and a half metres high occupied by people who were almost my size and whose expressions and movements had been caught in rainbow flashes of colour and intricate texture.

Whether it be standing before a painting, or sitting in a cinema, or listening to music being performed, or reading a novel, a number of different types of activities are taking place as we interact with a 'work of art'. We can summarise these interactions in this simple diagram.

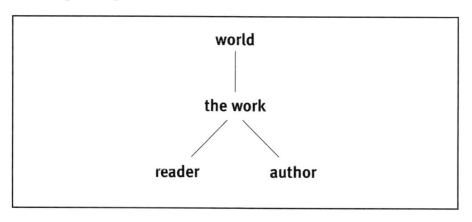

For example, as I contemplated Renoir's painting (let's call it 'the **work**'), it was possible to concentrate on the *subject* of the work (we'll call that its '**world**'). If this were my concern, I might try and work out the people or actions, ideas or feelings, things and events, that gave rise to such a painting.

Instead, I might treat the work in isolation, only being interested in the painting itself. In this case, I would concentrate on what it is made of, how it was composed and the use of colours and hues.

Alternatively, I might focus my attention on the **artist**. In this case, I would ask myself who he was and why he bothered painting this work. Perhaps some biographical information would give me insight to his motivations.

Lastly, I might come at the work from the perspective of what it does for me (that is, focus on the **audience**). How did I react when I first saw it? What memories does it spark in me? Do I relate strongly to it, or feel like it is very foreign to my experience?

These are all different ways of interacting with this work of art.

The same diagram, slightly amended, can be used to talk about how we approach a piece of literature, such as the books of the Bible. Before we think about the Bible itself, let's look at the following postcard I received recently:

> *Hi y'all! I'm writing as I wait to see how clouds will move. There are great mountains here, if only we can see them! Calvin's Geneva was inspiring: Paris was too much to see in a short stay. Chadwicks and I made it to Chartres for a day's outing. USA & Canada were full of natural beauty. I go tomorrow to London via Zurich. Am keeping well & the weary days are few. So much to see and reflect upon. Hope you had a good time with David C.*
>
> *Ken F*

Our slightly revised diagram would look like this:

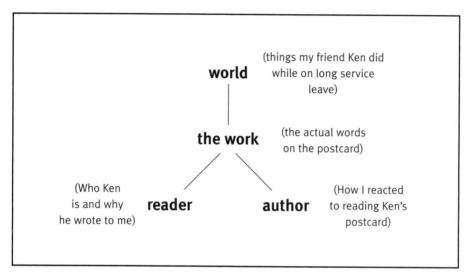

In this case, the **world** is the events that are spoken about (what Ken did). The **work** is the actual postcard itself and the words on it. The **author** is Ken F and the **reader** is firstly me (the original reader) and secondly you (the contemporary reader).

So, when we ask ourselves "What does this postcard mean?", it is possible to respond in a variety of ways. For example, we can say that its meaning lies with the subject being written about–it puts us in touch with the **world** of Ken's long service leave. We often take this sort of approach when we read a history book (e.g. a book telling us about the World War II).

We could also say that meaning lies with the text of the postcard itself (the '**work**'), that is, in the way it is put together, the form it takes, and the words it uses. Ken writes in short sentences, just communicating the main details. He uses colloquial language, suggesting a friendly tone. A poem studied in a schoolroom or tutorial setting often pays attention to these sorts of features.

Alternatively we might find meaning for the work in the **author's**–Ken's–reasons, motivations and intentions in writing the work. Was he trying to renew a friendship that had lapsed? Is he a great admirer of natural beauty, since he mentions these details? How does he know the 'Chadwicks', and why does he ask me about 'David C'? We often analyse personal letters in this way, trying to work out what they really convey about how the writer is feeling or thinking.

Lastly, we could focus upon what the words of the postcard mean for me (the **original reader**) or you (the **secondary reader**). For me, I felt like my friendship with Ken was being sustained. He was letting me in on what he was doing, so I felt good about the card. It made me want to travel to Geneva, to see the place where Calvin had made such an impact. I also know 'the Chadwicks', so I could imagine what it would have been like to join them on a 'day's outing'. Reading a novel is often like this—I read because I want the novel to affect me, to inspire me and to take me out of the mundane world of everyday existence.

It should be clear by now that the way you approach a 'work' greatly influences the sort of meaning you draw from your inter-action with it. You can take any or all of these approaches to the Bible. In the next section, I make some suggestions about which approaches are valid, and which approaches are dangerous when it comes to properly understanding the Scriptures.

Sympathetic reading

When we come to the Bible we need to be careful and cautious about how we read. And the first thing to be said that we should read the Bible 'sympathetically'. Reading sympathetically means reading it in light of its stated goals and purpose. Reading sym-pathetically also means reading in the light of how it presents itself. Let me explain.

First, the ultimate author of the Bible is God. Through his Holy Spirit he inspires people and they speak his word. Moreover, God speaks as a Creator to his creatures, seeking to reveal himself to them and seeking to draw out their response. This means that you can't treat it like an entertaining novel, or a piece of pleasant poetry. Our reading of the Bible must never be done in an abstract way, or keeping its message at arm's length. *Rather, our interpretation of the Bible must be done with an ear open to hear what God, the* **author**, *is saying and with a clear understanding that through the Scriptures God is making a claim upon us.*

Second, the Bible makes it clear that God regards words as very important to the process of revealing himself to us and making a claim upon us. He *speaks* in Scripture and the words he speaks are true and dependable. Throughout the Bible, God is certain that words can be understood with the mind. Words are at the centre of his revelation of himself. By implication, therefore, the words of the Bible itself—the **work**—is to occupy centre stage in our interpretation.

Nevertheless, that is not all. The God who is revealed in the Bible is not a distant God who is uninvolved in his world. He is a God who is passionately interested in what is happening in his world and with the people he has placed in the world. His revelation of himself does not occur in a vacuum. It is intimately connected with people and history. At times, the Bible explicitly draws our attention to this by naming the people and situations being talked about. God's revelation of himself is bound up with a **world** of people and events somewhat removed from us. Hence, there will be times when dipping into some more detail about the human author, his world and his intention in shaping the text in a particular way will aid and correct our understanding of the impact it should have on us.

Finally, when we read the Bible we do so with a vast world of personal experiences, presuppositions, ideas about life, interests and concerns. God knows us, and speaks to us today through these words written so long ago. His Holy Spirit, who inspired the writings in the first place, is at work in us. This interaction between God, the original author, and us, the **secondary readers**, is what God wants. It is the means he uses to speak to us. The impact that the text of Scripture has on us is, therefore, of great importance. However, it is an impact which must be tempered by our knowledge of the author—both human and divine, the world from which the Bible comes and the proper understanding of the words of the Bible itself. We cannot simply examine our reactions to the Bible and say that this is God speaking to us. In fact, this whole book has been trying to get us out of that bad habit.

In other words, when we approach the Bible, our part as **readers** is to *submit* to the authority of the **author**, the **work** and the biblical **world**. The 'baggage' we bring to understanding Scripture has to be brought under control by these other three elements. This is an unpopular view at the moment, but God requires no less.

bible translations

"Which version of the Bible should I use?".

The reminders of my struggle with this question still litter my bookshelves. When I first became a Christian in the mid-70s I knew the Bible was important. What I didn't know was that there was a multiplicity of versions of the Bible from which I could choose. What I also didn't know was that some versions were looked upon with favour and others looked upon with great disfavour, if not derision.

After some 20 years as a Christian, the situation hasn't greatly changed. The question of which version to use and how to choose between them remains. If we can put aside peer pressure for a moment, how do we decide which version is best? Is there such a thing as a better choice?

There is a lot that can be said to answer these questions. In this appendix, I'll examine just one of the key issues, then review a number of the major recent English translations before giving some tips on how to choose a version suitable for you.

Dynamic equivalence

Before looking at modern English translations it is important to understand one particular change in thinking regarding the whole process of translation. This change concerns a theory of translation known as 'dynamic equivalence'. It refers to an approach to translation in which one's chief concern is not to turn the original text into English *word-for-word*. Rather, the translator aims to translate *thought-for-thought*. With dynamic equivalence, the concern is with the *message* and its *meaning* rather than trying to replace each *word* with a similar word in English. Eugene Nida of the American Bible Society described the process in the following manner:

To translate is to try to stimulate in the new reader in the new language the same reaction to the text the original author wished to stimulate in the first and immediate readers.

An example of word-for-word translation is John 14:1 in the Revised Standard Version: "Let not your hearts be troubled". An example of the dynamic equivalence approach is found in the Good News Bible for the same passage: "Do not be worried or upset". The RSV sought to render the Greek text into English whereas the GNB tried to capture the original meaning of the phrase and provide a contemporary equivalent.

Understanding the dynamic equivalence approach will help us understand the differences between Bible translations.

Three previous standards

Three Bible translations had great influence up until the middle of this century: The Authorised (or King James) Version, The Revised Version and the Revised Standard Version.

The Authorised (King James) Version (1611)

Compiled by the best scholars in England under the patronage of King James I, the King James Version was authorised to be read in churches. It eventually replaced all of its contemporaries both in private and public use, and remained unchallenged until late in the 19th century. Although many people have hailed it as an example of the beauty and grandeur of the English language, others in its own day considered its language barbarous.

The KJV is still held by some to be *the* authoritative translation, although their reasoning is dubious to say the least.

The Revised Version (1881-85)

This translation was completed by a number of distinguished British scholars and based on the best available Greek and Hebrew texts. The New Testament translation was a big improvement on the KJV, since many of the manuscripts used had not been available in 1611. However, the Old Testament translation is not quite so competent.

The RV aimed to alter the KJV only where improved theological, textual or linguistic knowledge made this necessary. The result was a very reliable Bible for the times.

The Revised Standard Version (1946-52)

Americans had prepared their own version of the Revised Version (called, not surprisingly, the American Revised Version). This translation was later revised again by the National Council of Churches in America. The resulting Revised Standard Version made use of developments in scholarship and changes in English usage. The RSV has been criticised for not taking the dynamic equivalence approach to translation seriously. It retained too much archaic language ('thee' and 'thou') and did not adopt modern knowledge of wording and arrangement of passages. Nevertheless, it was a very popular Bible in the churches.

Major recent English translations

There are a great many translations now available. Below, I have outlined the rationale behind the most popular versions currently in use.

The Good News Bible (1966)

The Good News Bible is also known as Today's English Version. It is the first American attempt at a dynamic equivalence translation. Occasionally it is a little too free in departing from a literal rendering of the original. Its great advantage at publication was its simplicity and ease of reading. This quality opened up the Bible to many who had never read, and would never read, a version of the Bible couched in 16th century English (like the KJV).

Since publication of the GNB, however, there have been translations that are equally readable and which are not as free in translation. For this reason, I wouldn't generally recommend the GNB for regular use by the average Australian reader. It may, however, be a good introduction to the Bible for a young reader or a person for whom English is a new language.

The New American Standard Bible (1971)

This version of the Bible is a revision of the American Standard Version of 1901 and is the most literal, word-for-word translation on the market at present. It is a good study Bible for the sort of study advocated in this book but the language is a bit stilted and wooden for Australian readers wishing to read large slabs.

New International Version (1973)

The NIV has rapidly become the standard translation among evangelical Australian Christians, both as a pew Bible and for private use. The translation is midway between the RSV and the GNB, perhaps falling more on the side of the GNB and dynamic equivalence. This leaves it at a disadvantage as a study Bible since in order to convey meaning the translators sometimes make decisions regarding interpretation that a more literal translation leaves up to the reader.

For example, in Romans 1:16 the original Greek text reads literally, "a righteousness of God", which could mean either "God's own righteousness" or "a righteousness from God". This difference can have a significant impact on how you interpret Romans 1, if not the whole letter. Although both options for translation have major scholarly support, the NIV translators make the interpretative choice for you and translate the phrase "a righteousness from God". The decision is thereby taken out of the reader's hands at what turns out to be a very important and pivotal point in Paul's argument in Romans.

The number of complaints people have with the NIV seems to be growing.

The New Revised Standard Bible

The NRSV is an authorised revision of the RSV. It takes into account the most recent textual discoveries impinging on the Hebrew text of the Old Testament and the Greek of the New Testament. Its rule in translating has been "As literal as possible, as free as necessary". It therefore remains essentially a literal translation.

The translation reflects a modern use of English, so the archaic 'thee' and 'thou' of the RSV have disappeared. The NRSV's other primary characteristic is that it has adopted the use of inclusive language. For example, compare the RSV and NRSV translations of Hebrews 2:6-8.

> *What is man that thou art mindful of him,*
> *or the son of man, that thou carest for him? (RSV)*
>
> *What are human beings that you are mindful of them,*
> *or mortals, that you care for them? (NRSV)*

By taking out the phrase 'son of man' (presumably for reasons of 'sexism'), any possible allusion to Jesus is lost in the NRSV. In my view this is the main drawback of the translation. It tends to go overboard in a few places, opting for inclusive language when it might have been better to be more constrained. In other words, at times the principal of inclusive language has regrettably seemed to dominate its approach.

So which version?

Unless you can read the biblical languages, you are reliant upon translations of the Bible. The best way forward seems to be to have more than one translation. My criteria for choosing which version to use is as follows:

- When the Bible is being used for evangelistic purposes, head towards a freer, dynamic equivalence translation.
- When you are reading large slabs of the Bible in order to get a feel for the big picture, use a freer translation.
- When the Bible is being used for study purposes, head towards a more literal translation.

Hence, my first choice in choosing a Bible would be a more literal translation (e.g. NASB, RSV or NRSV) which has a good cross reference and concordance system attached. After this I would choose a translation which falls more on the side of

dynamic equivalence and modern language (the NIV in prefer-
ence to the GNB, which is probably too free in its translation).
This is the sort of translation I'd use to read large slabs of the
Bible and to get a feel for its overall story. It's also my current
choice as an evangelistic Bible.

On a final note, I need to say a word about Study Bibles and
their use. I do now have one Study Bible, but I purposefully leave
it in my library and use it only for reference, in the same way that
I'd use a Bible dictionary. As a rule of thumb, don't take a Study
Bible to a Bible study group. They are one of the best known
ways to short circuit good corporate grappling with the text of
Scripture. At a personal level, they are a danger because they
offer a constant temptation to laziness (i.e. to look in the margin
for explanation rather than doing the thinking and searching
yourself). Furthermore, there is an almost inevitable shift in your
attitude away from seeing the text of Scripture as being authoritative to treating the margin notes as being more authoritative.

About Matthias Media

Ever since 'St Matthias Press and Tapes' first opened its doors in 1988, under the auspices of St Matthias Anglican Church, Centennial Park, in Sydney, our aim has been to provide the Christian community with products of a uniformly high standard—both in their biblical faithfulness and in the quality of the writing and production.

Now known as Matthias Media, we have grown to become a nationwide provider of user-friendly resources for ministry, with Christians of all sorts using our Bible studies, books, Briefings, audio cassettes, videos, training courses—you name it.

For more information about the range of Matthias Media resources, call us on Freecall 1800 814 360 (or in Sydney 9663-1478), or fax us on (02) 9662-4289, and we will send you a free catalogue. Or you can e-mail us at sales@matthiasmedia.com.au. Or visit our Web site at: www.matthiasmedia.com.au

Buy direct from us and save

If you order your Matthias Media resources direct from us, you not only save time and money, you invest in more great resources for the future:

- you save time—we usually despatch our orders within 24 hours of receiving them

- you save money—our normal prices are better than other retailers' prices (plus if you order in bulk, you'll save even more)

- you help keep us afloat—because we get more from each sale, buying from us direct helps us to stay alive in the difficult world of publishing.

1800 814 360
or in Sydney:
(02) 9663 1478

Matthias Media
Reply Paid 225
Kingsford NSW 2032

(02) 9662 4289
(pay by credit
card or invoice)

Now that you've sharpened your Bible reading skills...

Our Interactive Bible Studies (IBS) and Topical Bible Studies (TBS) are a valuable resource to help you keep feeding from God's Word. The IBS series works through passages and books of the Bible; the TBS series pulls together the Bible's teaching on topics, such as money or prayer. As at June 2000, the series contains the following titles:

Beyond Eden
(Genesis 1-11)
Authors: Phillip Jensen and
Tony Payne, 9 studies

The One and Only
(Deuteronomy)
Author: Bryson Smith,
8 studies

Famine & Fortune
(Ruth)
Authors: Barry Webb and
David Hohne, 4 studies

The Eye of the Storm
(Job)
Author: Bryson Smith,
6 studies

Two Cities
(Isaiah)
Authors: Andrew Reid and
Karen Morris, 9 studies

Kingdom of Dreams
(Daniel)
Authors: Andrew Reid and
Karen Morris, 8 studies

Burning Desire
(Obadiah and Malachi)
Authors: Phillip Jensen and
Richard Pulley, 6 studies

Full of promise
(The Big Picture of the O.T.)
Authors: Phil Campbell
and Bryson Smith, 8 studies

The Good Living Guide
(Matthew 5:1-12)
Authors: Phillip Jensen and
Tony Payne, 9 studies

News of the Hour
(Mark)
Author: Peter Bolt,
10 studies

Free for All
(Galatians)
Authors: Phillip Jensen
and Kel Richards, 8 studies

Walk this Way
(Ephesians)
Author: Bryson Smith,
8 studies

The Complete Christian
(Colossians)
Authors: Phillip Jensen and
Tony Payne, 8 studies

To the Householder
(1 Timothy)
Authors: Phillip Jensen and
Greg Clarke, 9 studies

Run the Race
(2 Timothy)
Author: Bryson Smith,
6 studies

The Path to Godliness
(Titus)
Authors: Phillip Jensen and
Tony Payne, 6 studies

The Implanted Word
(James)
Authors: Phillip Jensen and
K.R. Birkett, 8 studies

Homeward Bound
(1 Peter)
Authors: Phillip Jensen and
Tony Payne, 10 studies

All You Need to Know
(2 Peter)
Author: Bryson Smith,
6 studies

Bold I Approach
(Prayer)
Author: Tony Payne,
6 studies

Cash Values
(Money)
Author: Tony Payne,
5 studies

The Blueprint
(Doctrine)
Authors: Phillip Jensen
and Tony Payne, 11 studies

Woman of God
(The Bible on Women)
Authors: Terry Blowes
8 studies